WOMEN REFUGEE VOICES FROM ASIA AND AFRICA

This book presents experiences of women refugees in a variety of contexts across Asia and Africa and builds a framework to ensure robust and effective mechanisms to safeguard refugees' rights. It highlights the structural challenges that women who are forcibly displaced face and the inadequacies of the response of governments and other stakeholders, irrespective of the country of origin, ethnicity, and religion of the refugee community.

This volume:

- Focuses on contemporary issues such as the Rohingya and the Syrian crisis.
- Brings first-person accounts of women refugees from Asia and Africa.
- Draws on an interdisciplinary approach to analyse a host of issues, including public policy, cultural norms, and economics of forced migration.

Bringing together first-hand accounts from women refugees and interventions by activists, academics, journalists, filmmakers, humanitarian workers, and international law experts, this book will be a must read for scholars and researchers of migration and diaspora studies, development studies, sociology and social anthropology, and politics and public policy. It will be of special interest to NGOs, policymakers, and think tanks.

ActionAid Association (AAA) is an organisation working for social and ecological justice. AAA has been engaged with the most marginalised communities in India since 1972. In 2006, it was registered as an Indian organisation, governed by an independent General Assembly and a Governing Board. Together with supporters, communities, institutions, and governments, it strives for equality, fraternity, and liberty for all.

ActionAid Association has been at the forefront of responding to the emergency needs of forcibly displaced communities for over four decades. AAA prioritises the needs of women and children and builds resilience of marginalised populations. AAA has supported displaced minorities from Pakistan living in Rajasthan, and internally displaced persons from Chhattisgarh settled in Andhra Pradesh. In partnership with the UN High Commissioner for Refugees, AAA extends support to people from the Rohingya community settled in parts of Uttar Pradesh and Haryana. AAA advocates for the universal rights of refugees, regardless of gender, class, caste, ethnicity, religion, and country of origin. AAA feels it is the collective responsibility of the international community to respond and ensure the rights of refugees.

WOMEN REFUGEE VOICES FROM ASIA AND AFRICA

Travelling for Safety

Edited by
ActionAid Association

LONDON AND NEW YORK

First published 2022
by Routledge
2 Park Square, Milton Park, Abingdon, Oxon OX14 4RN

and by Routledge
605 Third Avenue, New York, NY 10158

Routledge is an imprint of the Taylor & Francis Group, an informa business

© 2022 selection and editorial matter, ActionAid Association; individual chapters, the contributors

The right of ActionAid Association to be identified as the author of the editorial material, and of the authors for their individual chapters, has been asserted in accordance with sections 77 and 78 of the Copyright, Designs and Patents Act 1988.

All rights reserved. No part of this book may be reprinted or reproduced or utilised in any form or by any electronic, mechanical, or other means, now known or hereafter invented, including photocopying and recording, or in any information storage or retrieval system, without permission in writing from the publishers.

Trademark notice: Product or corporate names may be trademarks or registered trademarks, and are used only for identification and explanation without intent to infringe.

British Library Cataloguing-in-Publication Data
A catalogue record for this book is available from the British Library

Library of Congress Cataloging-in-Publication Data
A catalog record has been requested for this book

ISBN: 978-0-367-46971-9 (hbk)
ISBN: 978-0-367-49712-5 (pbk)
ISBN: 978-1-003-04709-4 (ebk)

DOI: 10.4324/9781003047094

Typeset in Bembo
by Deanta Global Publishing Services, Chennai, India

Visual on Cover: A sketch by Molly Crabapple

CONTENTS

Notes on contributors ix
Foreword xii
Acknowledgements xv

PART I
Overview   **1**

1 Introduction   3
 Divita Shandilya and Sandeep Chachra

 The special vulnerability of refugee women   5
 Crisis of identity and other themes   7
 Making refugees the object of discourse   8
 Notes   11

2 Forced displacement: Reflecting on women's lived realities   12
 Rebecca Eapen and Sweta Madhuri Kannan

 Overview   12
 Gender considerations in interpreting international refugee law   13
 Protection challenges faced by women and girls in forced
  displacement   14
 Strengthening strategies for change   16
 New ways of working: the Global Compact on Refugees   18
 Conclusion   19
 Notes   20

PART II
The path they travelled: Stories of refugee women — 23

3 Narratives of refugee women — 25
Bernadette Vivuya, Laith Marouf, Rosy Fernando, Samia Zennadi, Sharmin Akther Shilpi, and Universal Just and Action Society

    Stories of Rohingya women in Bangladesh — 26
    Stories from Sri Lankan Tamil women in India — 37
    Stories from Pakistani displaced minorities in India — 48
    Stories from West Saharan women in Algeria — 56
    Stories from refugee women in the Democratic Republic of Congo — 61
    Stories of internally displaced women in Syria — 66

4 A face to the journeys: From the pages of an artist's sketchbook — 72
Molly Crabapple

5 Rohingya exodus 2017: A photo essay on life at refugee camps in Cox's Bazar, Bangladesh — 90
Mahmud Rahman

6 Feminists on the move — 102
Priyali Sur

    Abeer — 102
    Shabana — 104
    Biba — 106
    On leaving home — 107
    Notes — 108

PART III
The particular vulnerabilities of refugee women — 109

7 Protection gaps for women and girls in refugee crises — 111
Jane Freedman

    Notes — 117

8 Social and cultural isolation of women in refuge — 118
Shahanoor Akter Chowdhury and Sharmin Akther Shilpi

    Introduction — 118
    Conflict, violence, and trauma — 119

Family separation in exile	120
Invisibility in the host country	121
Conclusion	123
Notes	126

9 Women, social positioning, and refugee status — 127
Rose Jaji

Introduction	127
The transience fallacy and host country fatigue	128
Refugee women and the difficulties they face	130
Exile and opportunities	132
Quest for self-reliance	133
Conclusion	134
Notes	135

10 Forced migration and the gendering of survival in exile — 136
Romola Sanyal

Introduction	136
Precarious lives: poverty and informality as key features of forced displacement	137
The gendered nature of work	141
Conclusion	143
Notes	144

PART IV
The contours of a long-term resolution — 147

11 Statelessness in exile — 149
Divita Shandilya

Making of statelessness	150
Stateless and displaced	152
Statelessness in abeyance	154
Conclusion	156
Notes	158

12 Refugee repatriation: The role of education, healthcare, livelihood, and violence — 160
Mollie Gerver

The role of education	160
The role of livelihoods	163
The role of healthcare	164

The role of domestic violence and conflict	165
Complex cases	166
Conclusion	167
Notes	167

13 Towards durable solutions: The rights of refugees and shared responsibilities of states to ensure their protection   169
Rebecca Dowd

Introduction	169
The international refugee law framework	170
Where it counts: Implementation of the international protection regime	172
Where to from here?	173
Notes	175

Index   177

NOTES ON CONTRIBUTORS

Editors

Divita Shandilya works with ActionAid Association as Programme Manager of Policy and Research. She has a Master's in International Relations and works on issues of public policy and human rights from the perspective of the Global South.

Divita has a deep interest in issues of gender, migration, displacement, and South–South cooperation. She has worked extensively on women's socio-economic and political rights. She is a member of several international feminist alliances and is also active in civil society advocacy spaces of multilateral fora such as BRICS, G20, and CSW, particularly on women's rights.

Sandeep Chachra serves as Executive Director of ActionAid Association and is a social anthropologist by training. He has been working in the arena of social development for the last three decades, in India and globally.

Sandeep is one of the founders of the Agrarian South Network and South–South Peoples Solidarity Forum and works with a range of people's formations in different countries in pursuit of social and ecological justice. Currently, he is the Managing Editor of a leading global political economy journal on agrarian and work questions, called Agrarian South.

Sandeep Chachra is also Co-Chair of the World Urban Campaign of the UN-HABITAT.

Contributors

Shahanoor Akter Chowdhury is Gender Mainstreaming Specialist, Save the Children International-Rohingya Response, Bangladesh. She previously worked as Women's Rights and Protection Coordinator with ActionAid Bangladesh – Rohingya Response programme.

Molly Crabapple is an artist and writer. She is the author of *Drawing Blood* and *Brothers of the Gun* (with Marwan Hisham), which was nominated for a National Book Award in 2018. Her work is in the permanent collection of the Museum of Modern Art.

Rebecca Dowd is an international human rights lawyer, with particular expertise in refugee law. She has worked for UNHCR in Switzerland and Jordan, conducted academic research, and worked in the government and not-for-profit sectors. She currently works in disability policy and research.

Rebecca Eapen is currently UNHCR's Senior Adviser on Gender Equality. She has worked for over 15 years on gender equality, gender-based violence, and human rights issues in humanitarian and development contexts, including India, Sri Lanka, Nepal, Afghanistan, Timor Leste, and South Africa.

Rosy Fernando is founder and CEO, Startup Solutions, Chennai, India.

Jane Freedman is Professor of Politics at the Université de Paris 8, where she leads major international research projects on asylum and migration and violence against women. Recent publications include *Gendering the International Asylum and Refugee Debate* (Palgrave Macmillan, 2015) and *A Gendered Approach to the Syrian Refugee Crisis* (Routledge, 2017).

Mollie Gerver is Assistant Professor in Political Theory at the University of Essex and the author of *The Ethics and Practice of Refugee Repatriation*.

Rose Jaji is Senior Lecturer in the Department of Sociology at the University of Zimbabwe. Her research areas of interest are migration/refugees, gender, conflict, and peacebuilding. Her latest publication is a book titled *Deviant Destinations: Zimbabwe and North to South Migration*.

Sweta Madhuri Kannan leads on multi-stakeholder engagement in UNHCR's Global Refugee Forum Coordination Team. She has accompanied the consultation process for the New York Declaration (2016) and the Global Compact on Refugees (2018). She has been with UNHCR for seven years, including in Afghanistan, Yemen, and Europe.

Laith Marouf is a senior journalist based in West Asia.

Mahmud Rahman is a documentary photographer working on social issues. As a visual advocacy campaigner in Bangladesh, he uses his work to raise awareness through photo exhibitions and participatory workshops with selected groups in rural and urban areas, especially targeting the youth.

Romola Sanyal is Associate Professor of Urban Geography at the London School of Economics. Her work focuses on forced migration and urbanisation, particularly in the Global South.

Sharmin Akther Shilpi is Officer, Humanitarian Response, Resilience and Climate Justice Programme, ActionAid Bangladesh.

Priyali Sur is an international development professional and an independent multimedia journalist. In both spheres, her work focuses on social justice and gender issues. She has extensively covered the refugee crisis from Europe and the Middle East.

Bernadette Vivuya is an independent journalist and filmmaker based in Goma, in Eastern DRC. She works on human rights, the environment, and minerals exploitation. She has a particular interest in subjects that bear witness to the resilience of the population of this region affected by many conflicts.

Samia Zennadi is an archaeologist by training, a publisher, and author of a book on the art of carpeting in Algeria. She is responsible for "L'Espace Panaf" at the 15th International Book Fair of Algiers during which she initiated a literary magazine *L'Afrique parle livres* (Africa speaks books). She is currently planning an anniversary event in Algeria to commemorate the 1973 Nonaligned Summit.

Universal Just and Action Society, Jodhpur, India, works with marginalised segments of society, including displaced Pakistani minority immigrants.

FOREWORD

I was 17 years old when war broke out in Liberia. I had just graduated from high school and dreamed of becoming a doctor. When the fighting started, my childhood virtually vanished overnight, and I became an adult responsible for taking care of my family. The whole world changed, but not just for me. Over the 14 years from 1989 to 2003, around 250,000 people were killed, 1 million were internally displaced, and 500,000 sought protection in refugee camps.

We fled to Ghana on a cargo ship filled with thousands of people. We arrived at Buduburam refugee camp with nothing. My mother made mattresses out of grass that she cut, dried, and stuffed into vegetable sacks so that we had something to sleep on. While my mother was a dispensing pharmacist, she was not allowed to practice her profession in Ghana. Instead, she sold vegetables, I fried doughnuts, and my sister managed the medical records for the camp's small medical clinic – each of us doing what we could to look after our family in the camp. Before long, I returned to Liberia.

In 1996, I again fled to Ghana, this time with my two children and five months pregnant. We travelled on board a ship called the *Bulk Challenge*. The *Bulk Challenge* made international headlines when Ghana refused to allow the ship to dock, saying that the international community was failing to assist with the refugee crisis. Conditions on the ship were desperate, and many passengers were ill, including me. After days of negotiations we were allowed to dock in Takroadi, Ghana. I later moved to Accra to live with the family of my children's father. I gave birth to my third child, nicknamed Birdie, a baby boy weighing just two pounds. Given that we were refugees but with no official refugee status and no cash, we were placed on the floor in the hospital hallway and my premature baby was never placed in the incubator he so clearly needed. Somehow he survived, and I also survived my severe case of anaemia.

I recently visited a Syrian refugee camp in Jordan. It made memories of my own refugee experience come rushing back. Talking with the young girls who are dreaming about education and leaving that space for a better life reminded me of the 17-year-old Leymah who dreamed of having her home and community back, just as it was. I also observed the lost look on the faces of adults who reminded me of my own mother sitting and wondering many days aloud about the state of our land. She would repeatedly say as if in a dream, "But Liberians were not evil people, what happened to us? How did we get here?" I could almost hear these older Syrians say the same thing as they stared in space.

I often tell anyone who will listen that no one wakes up and decides to leave everything that is familiar to them and become a refugee. Wars and increased violence cause many to make the most difficult and uncomfortable decision: leaving the known and familiar for the unknown and unfamiliar.

As an activist who now has the opportunity to visit refugee camps and also engage with refugees living outside of the camp setting, I notice that the infrastructure of refugee camps has not significantly improved in the 30 years since I was a refugee. Though some gains have been made, a lot still needs to happen around the daily lives and futures of refugees. In 1990, when we first arrived in Ghana, no one considered menstrual hygiene for women and girls; today that has changed. Food and other humanitarian aid were delivered without consideration to the traditional meals of refugees. Today, we can say some of these things are happening. However, camps are built in response to chaos, rather than being able to take into consideration how people live their lives. Host countries rarely allow refugees to practice their professions, and many people turn to manual labour to support themselves. Education opportunities are limited, if they exist at all. And for all the policy conversations about understanding the protection needs of women and girls, displacement significantly increases the risk of gender-based violence.

Once again, I returned to Liberia from Ghana. Amidst the fighting, life continued. A ceasefire was signed in 1997, and there were democratic elections. But within two years there was renewed fighting and Liberia was once again at war with itself. Many Liberians experienced displacement multiple times – fleeing and returning to Ghana or seeking refuge at camps in Liberia. As the war raged on, civilians sheltering in camps for internally displaced persons (IDPs) were increasingly the target of attack by all parties to the conflict.

It has been almost 30 years since my family and I first left home for safety in another land. I wish I could say our family was the last to experience such pain. Today, many more families are on the move as a result of war and or climate crises.

It seems to me that the conversation about refugees is stuck in meeting rooms, talking about policies, plans, and bureaucracies. It is time for the world to bring the human person to the centre of this discourse. Refugees are not statistics; they are humans with ambitions and dreams.

We must forge new paths for our daughters and sons. We can no longer justify having conversations about forced displacement without the leadership of those who have suffered the consequences of conflict and persecution. For too long, women and girls who are refugees or IDPs have been excluded from systems of representation and participation. But it is their lives that are being examined. And it is their voices that we must amplify.

Leymah Gbowee
Peace Activist and 2011 Nobel Peace Laureate
Founder & President of Gbowee Peace Foundation Africa

ACKNOWLEDGEMENTS

This important and timely book was made possible by the efforts of several people spread across different cities and continents. Divita Shandilya and Sandeep Chachra, ActionAid Association, held the entire project together from the start to the finish. Divita's unyielding commitment has seen the efforts of all coming together in the form of this book. Sandeep's belief in the cause of refugees and protecting their rights helped propel the project and provide it direction.

The project got its wings in great part due to Sehjo Singh, then with ActionAid Association and now with Industree Foundation. Sehjo's initial ideas were critical to the evolution of the project. The International Humanitarian Action and Resilience Team of ActionAid International, and Richard Miller, Lucy Blown, and Amar Jyoti Nayak, in particular, contributed greatly with crucial funding and much appreciated moral support.

Inputs from Samia Zennadi, APIC Editions, Dr Elisa T. Bertuzzo, Weissensee Academy of Art, Berlin, Carol Angir, ActionAid Australia, and Debabrat Patra, ActionAid Association were key in designing the framework and finalising the methodology. The project gained immensely from field visits to Rajasthan, India, and Cox's Bazar, Bangladesh. Hindu Singh Sodha, Ashok Suthar, and their team at Universal Just Action Society, as well as colleagues at ActionAid Bangladesh, hosted teams who interacted with refugees at these locations.

Samia Zennadi, APIC Editions; Bernadette Vivuya, Independent Journalist and Filmmaker; Laith Marouf, Geo-political Analyst and Media and Law Consultant; Dr Rosy Fernando, Founder and CEO, Startup Solutions; Sharmin Akther Shilpi, ActionAid Bangladesh; and Manisha Chouhan, Universal Just Action Society, spent many days in camps and settlements talking to refugee women and reporting their narratives with both empathy and objectivity, qualities which are becoming rarer by the day. Nirja Bhatnagar, Esther Mariaselvam, and Narendra Sharma of ActionAid Association and Feroze Mithiborwala, Peace

Activist and General Secretary, India Palestine Solidarity Forum, deserve special mention for their support in coordinating the field work.

Varsha Rani Tirkey, Nabajit Malakar, and others in the communications team of ActionAid Association provided support to this project in uncountable ways. Joseph Mathai was instrumental in ensuring that this book saw the light of day. Gratitude is due to Diksha Sood and Ellie Thompson who interned with ActionAid Association during the project and collected background information, helped in the production of the book, and edited its initial drafts. Shalini Garg and Varshlata Rohida, and others in the finance team of ActionAid Association, made sure that the project could run smoothly.

Sharmila Chandra provided valuable copy-editing support, vastly improving the typescript. Aakash Chakrabarty, Shoma Choudhury, Brinda Sen, and the rest of the team at Routledge have been incredibly helpful during the entire process.

The contributing authors have brought a depth of experience and expertise to this project and have enriched it manifold. They put up with multiple demands and numerous revisions and have been extremely gracious and involved through the process. Leymah Gbowee, peace activist and Nobel Laureate, most willingly wrote the foreword, which starts off this book on a powerful note. Finally, and most importantly, all of us concerned with this project thank the refugee women who have opened up their hearts and hearths to us and trusted us with their personal experiences and precious and often painful memories.

PART I
Overview

1
INTRODUCTION

Divita Shandilya and Sandeep Chachra

We are at a critical juncture in history where the number of people who have been forcibly displaced from their homes is the highest it has ever been. At the end of 2020, 82.4 million people had been forcibly displaced due to war, violence, persecution, and disasters, including 48 million internally displaced persons (IDPs) and 26.4 million refugees.[1] In their search for safety, these people are increasingly facing highly militarised borders, hostile government policies, and unfriendly local populations.

The global refugee system seems to be failing them as it struggles to cope with the challenges of large-scale displacements, mixed migration flows of asylum seekers, refugees, stateless persons, and migrants, and protracted situations of conflict and displacement. Moreover, a growing number of people, including displaced women and children and refugees living in slums in urban areas, are unable to access the protection and support mechanisms set up under this system.

These shortcomings are the result of years of ineffective governance due to a lack of political will, absence of accountability, inadequate responsibility sharing, and insufficient and inefficient funding. In a deeper sense, these shortcomings are also rooted in global and national economic development trajectories which continue to create an extreme concentration of wealth at the one end, and masses of dispossessed people living in poverty and assetlessness at the other end. The World Refugee Council has characterised this crisis aptly: "Our world suffers not so much from a refugee crisis as from a political crisis – a deficit of leadership and vision and, most fundamentally, a shortfall of humanity and empathy."[2]

The crisis has extracted a huge cost from forcibly displaced persons. It constantly undermines their physical security and mental well-being. The material deprivation of asylum seekers and refugees becomes more entrenched in most cases, with few opportunities for future generations to improve their conditions. Their rights are curtailed and denied in various ways, relegating them to the margins of society. In this context, there is an urgent need to critically engage with current refugee policies and reshape them based on the lived experiences of refugees.

This book presents to its readers these experiences in the form of narratives from women refugees. The introductory chapter authored by Rebecca Eapen and Sweta Madhuri Kannan reflects on international legal protections and support mechanisms and how they could be better utilised and expanded to protect the rights of refugees. Part II of this book presents stories of women travelling for refuge, captured in narrative accounts, sketches, and photographs of women in refugee camps across Asia and Africa. These two continents generate and host the largest number of refugees in the world.

The narratives cover relatively recent situations of mass displacement such as in Syria and Bangladesh. It also looks at protracted conditions of Tamil Sri Lankan refugees and displaced Hindus from Pakistan in India, Western Saharan refugees in Algeria, and refugees from Burundi, Rwanda, and Uganda living in the Democratic Republic of Congo (DRC).

Part III explores varied themes related to refuge and being a refugee. These include the challenges faced by people in accessing safety at the time of displacement and their struggles and survival strategies in displacement. Part IV looks at issues of integration, relocation, and repatriation of refugees, and explores their trepidations and hopes and attempts to draw out the contours of the needed resolution.

The rampant misgovernance has been fuelled by public apathy, which in turn is stoked and exploited by politicians who are wont to whipping up paranoia for short-term gains, often through falsehoods and exaggerations. We see this in the way that far-right populist and nationalist parties have gained credence across the world. They may have different roots and trajectories but are united by their anti-immigration stance and the strikingly similar language and tools that they deploy to garner support. At the receiving end are asylum seekers and migrants.

There is a manifold increase in institutionalised racism and xenophobia against displaced populations. They are being routinely denied asylum, detained, subjected to violence, and sent back to countries that they have fled, with little regard for their security and well-being. Riding on the back of increasing inequalities, contracting opportunities, and lack of jobs, rising chauvinistic "sons of the soil" tendencies are further pushing displaced people into precarity. Governments and people have become too narrowly focused on highlighting those aspects of a displaced person's identity that they perceive as a threat, be it religion, race, ethnicity, or country of origin, and excluding them for it. In the exclusion of others, people appear to reaffirm their own sense of belongingness.

There is also a tendency, an emphasis almost, on grading the trauma and suffering of displaced people to determine who among them deserves asylum and who does not. Distinctions in circumstances certainly exist, which merit differing levels of protection for different groups. But asylum policies and procedures have today morphed into laborious exercises to qualify whether one is a refugee or an immigrant, often through extremely narrow prisms. This is the case even as governments are constraining the legal pathways to migration and asylum and attempting to delegitimise the presence of existing populations within their territory, especially from minority communities. Through all these extremely fraught and contested processes, the voices of refugees remain unheard and ignored.

But the narratives of otherisation and vilification need to be countered. The representation of refugees in media and popular imagination should be supplemented by stories which speak truthfully to their circumstances, to the difficult choices that they have had to make, to their motivations, and to their hopes and aspirations. Refugees have had their humanity chipped away little by little by people refusing to engage with their experiences and by the constant undermining of their agency. We must help in restoring this sense of agency by listening to them.

This book intends to facilitate this process by bringing voices of refugee women to the fore, whose issues and needs are often sidelined. By focusing on their stories, we wish to bring out the individuality of their experiences, which often get lost in a bucket of generalisations. At the same time, we hope that readers would appreciate the commonalities in their situations across religions, race, ethnicities, and nationalities; there seems to be a lot more in common than that which divides.

The special vulnerability of refugee women

Women and girls make up an estimated 50 per cent of all forcibly displaced people worldwide.[3] It is widely agreed that they are extremely vulnerable in displacement contexts. The everyday structural discrimination and violence that women and girls face across the world gets further exacerbated in times of conflict and displacement. They are often targeted for sexual abuse and exploitation and face rampant gender-based violence, with little recourse to authorities and legal mechanisms. In addition, they are denied or are unable to access services and resources as well as education and job opportunities. When people are forcibly displaced, and resources and opportunities are at a premium, women and girls are usually the first ones to bear the brunt.

It is widely acknowledged that addressing vulnerabilities specific to women is central to effective responses to refugee movements. There are several international resolutions which emphasise the need to enhance protection for refugee women and girls and enable them as independent actors. The Conclusion on Refugee Women adopted by the Executive Committee of the United Nations High Commissioner for Refugees (UNHCR) in its 39th session in 1988, for example, elaborates on the special vulnerability of refugee women and the problems they face, notably in the area of physical security. It calls for the need to promote the participation of refugee women as agents as well as beneficiaries of programmes on their behalf.[4] More recently, the Global Compact on Refugees adopted by the United Nations General Assembly states that women and girls may experience particular gender-related barriers that call for an adaptation of responses in the context of large refugee situations.[5]

Yet standard policy approaches to refugee situations have been largely homogenising. They do not consider the differential needs and circumstances of women, sexual minorities, children, and persons with disabilities. This allows for discrimination, exclusion, and violence based on gender, sexuality, caste, class, ability, and other similar factors which may exist within refugee populations to be ignored or worsen. It also leads to the invisibilisation of certain sections of the population to a system which by design cannot see them, thereby depriving them of access to aid, education, healthcare, and livelihoods. For example, in most refugee responses, registration to receive aid and other services is done in the name of the head of the household, typically a male member, regardless of the power dynamic within the household which can be critical in determining whether women can access these services.

When we talked to the refugee women, the detrimental effects of gaps in protection policies and welfare programmes were laid bare. These women belong to different age groups and are of diverse nationalities, religions, and ethnicities, but their experiences in displacement are remarkably similar. They have faced tremendous atrocities and hardships, both in the process of fleeing to safety and seeking asylum and while living in camps or slum-like situations in new countries.

They remain at high risk of intimate partner violence as well as sexual and gender-based violence by other men from within the communities or from local populations in host countries. They are very likely to be excluded from decision-making spaces due to societal constraints and patriarchal norms and because they are not seen as being representative of their communities. In situations where women are keen to or have been pushed into taking leadership roles by their circumstances, for instance in the case of women who may have lost their husbands in conflict, they are not provided the avenues and means to fulfil them.

Most of the women we spoke with do not have access to decent livelihoods and their families are either entirely dependent on aid or on the meagre incomes of the male head of the household. This further impedes the choices and freedoms available to women. They and their families are thus trapped in a cycle of poverty and violence that is not only pernicious for women but even for the families and communities. Despite being out of the dire straits that forced them to move, they are beset by a near-constant state of uncertainty and anxiety about whether their future generations might lead better lives.

The book delves into each of these aspects. It provides readers an opportunity to understand the various facets of refugee issues through a gendered lens. The narratives are based on semi-structured interviews enabling women to share their experiences in detail. And the deep dive into each story hopefully lets the reader discern the universal – in terms of what is shared – and that which is unique about each experience.

Crisis of identity and other themes

The narratives of refugee women form Chapter 3 of this book. Based on their stories and the recurring themes that were brought up, our contributing authors have written chapters that speak to these issues. They have drawn upon their expertise and fieldwork in countries as varied as Syria, Iraq, Lebanon, Afghanistan, Niger, Kenya, and South Sudan.

Chapters 4 and 5 are visual chapters. In Chapter 4, Molly Crabapple's sketches document the families of Kurdish Syrian refugees and the work of Doctors Without Borders/Médecins Sans Frontières (MSF) at the Domiz camp in Iraqi Kurdistan. In Chapter 5, Mahmud Rahman presents the plight of Rohingya refugees in the camps of Cox's Bazar in Bangladesh in the early days of the mass exodus of August 2017.

In their stories, women share their experiences of profound loss. They had to leave behind their homes, their possessions and were often separated from their family members. Some would be reunited with them in the camps but most of them were not so fortunate. Their journeys were undertaken in highly dangerous circumstances and generally in a clandestine manner due to the lack of safe migration routes and lack of awareness, documents, and money.

In Chapter 6, Priyali Sur explores the reasons which forced women to flee, the difficult journeys that they had to undertake, and the brutality they were subjected to by traffickers, smugglers, and border guards. Dr Jane Freedman elaborates on the structural and systemic gender inequalities before, during, and after forced displacement, which put women and girls at risk in Chapter 7.

The women highlight the near permanence of the state of displacement. Several refugee families report living in refugee camps and settlements in host countries for multiple generations. Some of the women interviewed were born in the camps and have continued living there for more than three decades. Among refugees mired in such protracted situations, it is also common to hear stories where people have been displaced more than once – either having to move from one area to another within the host country or from one country to another.

As these women struggle to get their lives together, the scars of violence and displacement are extremely visible. Their families and communities have been physically and emotionally damaged and the women are especially traumatised by the sexual violence that they were witness to or subjected to. Their situation is made worse by the multiple forms of vulnerabilities that they face. Insecurity and destitution have become endemic to their lives.

Chapter 8 authored by Shahanoor Akter Chowdhury and Sharmin Akther Shilpi focuses on the isolation that women face in displacement as a result of family separation in exile, gender-based discrimination and violence, and long-term trauma of war. In Chapter 9, Dr Rose Jaji brings in the dimension of women's material deprivation due to a combination of their low social position in many cultural contexts and their refugee status.

We also see similar stories of deprivation from women from the host community in Bangladesh. Their lives have been upended by the massive refugee inflow in the last couple of years, leading to restrictions in access to land, forest, water, and basic services, increase in commodity prices, increase in labour market competition, and downward pressure on wages. The poorest and the most marginalised among the host population have been hit the hardest.

In Chapter 10, Dr Romola Sanyal talks about the coping tactics that people adopt in such circumstances. They, especially women, are increasingly dependent on highly casualised forms of labour, but while informality of work offers people opportunity, it locks them into low-paying and precarious jobs.

It is common for refugee women and men to experience a crisis of identity, of not knowing their place in the world. Many refugees are born and have grown up in host countries. They have established social circles and set up a semblance of a stable life. They have received some form of education and training and may even have jobs. Yet they are unable to shake off the feeling of being stateless. They are very aware that they are outsiders to the host country, which is compounded by the fact that they have few rights and entitlements in the host country. In Chapter 11, Divita Shandilya examines the specific challenges that people who are stateless face in asylum. This includes those who are forced to flee due to their statelessness and those who are rendered stateless due to displacement.

Many women shared the feeling of being stuck in limbo. It is difficult for them to think of going back to their country as the situation remains volatile in most cases, with the threat of violence breaking out again looming large. For others, the fear of uprooting their lives and moving again is very daunting. Some of them are wary of going back as they are still pained and haunted by memories of war and the violence they endured. In most cases, the enabling infrastructure for repatriation does not exist, so even if they want to go back to their homeland, they are afraid to do so. Dr Mollie Gerver explores the multiple and complex factors that determine whether refugees choose to stay, repatriate, or relocate and how much agency they have in making these decisions in Chapter 12.

The stories point to a broader issue – displacement is not a single event that ends with return. It is an event that can occur multiple times, each time exposing affected people to new risks and challenges.

In the final chapter, Rebecca Dowd re-examines the international legal framework to draw out durable solutions to the issue of refugees and the right to refuge.

Making refugees the object of discourse

What these women want is to be able to earn a living, to feel safe in camps, to be able to access education for their children, and healthcare for their families. They want to be able to lead a dignified life without fear of being harassed by authorities or of being detained or arrested.

The international community has attempted to come together and address these concerns and move forward. In adopting the Global Compact, member states of the United Nations committed themselves to easing pressures on host countries, enhancing refugee self-reliance, expanding access to third country solutions, and supporting conditions in countries of origin for safe and dignified return.[6]

The New York Declaration on Refugees and Migrants has also asked countries to review policies which criminalise borders and detain asylum seekers while their applications are being processed and to work towards ending the practice of detaining children.[7]

Despite countries reiterating their commitment to refugees, the most divisive systemic issues persist. There is still no agreement on how countries will share the responsibility of hosting refugees, including financing in the short and long term, and how governments would be held accountable for their obligations. Given that 85 per cent of the world's refugees are concentrated in low- and middle-income countries, the pressure on the system is immense. But the total population of refugees is only 0.35 per cent of the global population, and, therefore, refugee sharing arrangements would greatly assist in releasing this pressure.

There are promising signs. In recent years, a few governments have adopted innovative policies to accommodate and integrate refugees, including facilitating their absorption in the formal workforce. Some countries have also experimented with regional models, aligning their policies with those of their neighbouring countries to ensure better policy outcomes. Furthermore, there is a fair amount of research happening on the ground in refugee camps and at the sites of displacement, analysing what works and what does not. A combination of these policies and learnings adapted to local conditions and to the needs of communities could help attempts to transform the system along.

In his work, for example, Alexander Betts focuses on the impossible choices that refugees are presented with, including encampment, usually in bleak locations with very limited prospects, urban destitution, or perilous journeys. He then presents ideas for expanding their choices through enabling environments, which include access to education, connectivity, electricity, transportation, capital, and livelihoods, and setting up economic zones which allow refugees to work. He also talks of a preference matching model which would enable refugees' destination preferences to be matched with state preferences based on certain factors such as skills and languages. He explores the idea of providing humanitarian visas as a legal means for asylum seekers to travel and avoid irregular, perilous journeys.[8]

On the other hand, the World Refugee Council is pushing for the institutional transformation of the refugee regime, beginning with the setting up of a Global Action Network for the Forcibly Displaced. They have also suggested that the norms for refugee response be reiterated and expanded through the development of an additional protocol to the 1951 Refugee Convention and an evidence collection body be established in the form of an Intergovernmental Panel on

Refugees and Displaced Persons. On the questions of accountability and finance, the council has recommended repurposing seized assets from regimes whose actions have forced people to flee and using them for the benefit of affected people and establishing new forms of financing such as refugee sovereign bonds and equity investment funds.[9]

The refugee system needs to be more responsive and decentralised with a robust partnership between refugee communities, governments, private sector, media, and civil society. It needs to evolve in conjunction with better migration policies as the violation of the human rights of migrants has a cascading effect on other groups on the move. All migration must be in safe and dignified conditions. And people who are displaced due to persecution, conflict, or environmental degradation must be provided special protection in the form of safe escape routes, access to asylum-seeking processes, first aid and life-saving assistance, housing, and other basic services such as education and healthcare, and livelihood support.

Good refugee policies are politically, economically, strategically, and morally defensible. Politically, if governments manage their borders well and establish transparent mechanisms to accept, process, and resettle refugees, they can prevent refugee inflows from rising to crisis proportions and assuage any fear among their citizens. Their willingness to respond in this manner is also a signal to other countries, particularly their neighbours, and can induce positive incentives for cooperation. Economically, the effective integration of forcibly displaced people can contribute to economic development in the host country, and alleviate potential costs associated with providing infrastructure, services, and resources in camp conditions.[10] Strategically, the resolution of conflict situations can depend on finding durable solutions for displaced populations. A swift and efficient response to refugee movements can also be vital to maintaining peace and security in the neighbourhood as most refugees flee to neighbouring countries for asylum. Morally, the protection of persecuted, conflict-affected people is one of the basic tenets of humanity. To deny them asylum and sufficient assistance to live in dignity and security is a violation of fundamental human rights.[11]

At the heart of these policies should be the millions of refugees who are looking for protection and for a chance to rebuild their lives. We need to see them more clearly and hear their stories more closely. The more stories we listen to, the more we challenge our prejudices.

As Hannah Arendt once wrote:

> The world is not humane just because it is made by human beings, and it does not become humane just because the human voice sounds in it, but only when it has become the object of discourse. However much we are affected by the things of the world, however deeply they may stir and stimulate us, they become human for us only when we can discuss them with our fellows. We humanize what is going on in the world and in ourselves

only by speaking of it, and in the course of speaking of it we learn to be human.[12]

Our effort through this book is to bring the world of refugees in its human dimension to you.

Notes

1 Figures at a Glance, UNHCR. Available at https://www.unhcr.org/figures-at-a-glance.html. Accessed on June 20, 2021.
2 A Call to Action, Transforming the Global Refugee System, World Refuge Council, 2019. Available at https://www.worldrefugeecouncil.org/sites/default/files/documents/WRC_Call_to_Action.pdf. Accessed on November 2, 2019.
3 UN Women, The Centrality of Gender Equality and Women's Empowerment for the Formulation of the Global Compact for Refugees. Available at https://www.unhcr.org/59ddff717.pdf. Accessed on May 10, 2021.
4 UNHCR Policy on Refugee Women, 1990. Available at https://www.unhcr.org/protection/women/3ba6186810/unhcr-policy-on-refugee-women-1990.html. Accessed on November 3, 2019.
5 Global Compact on Refugees, 2018. Available at https://www.unhcr.org/gcr/GCR_English.pdf. Accessed on November 3, 2019.
6 Global Compact on Refugees, 2018. Available at https://www.unhcr.org/gcr/GCR_English.pdf. Accessed on November 3, 2019.
7 New York Declaration for Refugees and Migrants, Resolution adopted by the General Assembly during its 71st session on 19 September 2016. Available at https://www.un.org/en/ga/search/view_doc.asp?symbol=A/RES/71/1. Accessed on November 1, 2019.
8 Alexander Betts, 2016. Our Refugee System Is Failing: Here's How We Can Fix It, *Ted Talk*. Available at https://www.ted.com/talks/alexander_betts_our_refugee_system_is_failing_here_s_how_we_can_fix_it/transcript?language=en. Accessed on October 30, 2019.
9 A Call to Action, Transforming the Global Refugee System, World Refuge Council, 2019. Available at https://www.worldrefugeecouncil.org/sites/default/files/documents/WRC_Call_to_Action.pdf. Accessed on November 2, 2019.
10 A Call to Action, Transforming the Global Refugee System, World Refuge Council, 2019. Available at https://www.worldrefugeecouncil.org/sites/default/files/documents/WRC_Call_to_Action.pdf. Accessed on November 2, 2019.
11 A Call to Action, Transforming the Global Refugee System, World Refuge Council, 2019. Available at https://www.worldrefugeecouncil.org/sites/default/files/documents/WRC_Call_to_Action.pdf. Accessed on November 2, 2019.
12 Hannah Arendt, 1968. On Humanity in Dark Times: Thoughts Lessing, *Men in Dark Times*.

2
FORCED DISPLACEMENT

Reflecting on women's lived realities[1]

Rebecca Eapen and Sweta Madhuri Kannan

> Certainly there are very real differences between us of race, age, and sex. But it is not those differences between us that are separating us. It is rather our refusal to recognize those differences.
>
> Audre Lorde[2]

Overview

While the history of international protection of refugees can be traced back through time, the most significant developments in the refugee protection regime are linked to the two world wars and the emergence of the international human rights law framework. The 1951 Convention relating to the Status of Refugees was developed after World War II. This was preceded by the UN General Assembly adopting the 1950 Statute of the Office of the UN High Commissioner for Refugees (UNHCR).

The 1951 Refugee Convention, its 1967 Protocol, which lifted time and geographic restrictions in the 1951 Convention, regional instruments including the 1969 Organization of African Unity (OAU) Convention governing Specific Aspects of Refugee Problems in Africa, the 1984 Cartagena Declaration on Refugees, and the Common European Asylum System are key instruments that together create the international protection framework for refugees.

The 1951 Convention defines a refugee as someone who is unable or unwilling to return to their country of nationality or habitual residence owing to a well-founded fear of being persecuted for reasons of race, religion, nationality, membership of a particular social group, or political opinion. The 1951 Convention also has a guarantee of protection from *non-refoulement* and a catalogue of civil, political, economic, social, and cultural rights.[3]

The international protection framework for refugees was further strengthened through the unanimous adoption of the New York Declaration for Refugees and Migrants in 2016.[4] The Declaration reaffirms the importance of the international refugee regime and contains a wide range of commitments by UN member states to strengthen and enhance mechanisms to protect people who have been forced to move. It paved the way for the adoption of two new global compacts in 2018: the Global Compact on Safe, Orderly and Regular Migration, and the Global Compact on Refugees.

Gender considerations in interpreting international refugee law

The 1951 Convention, written at a time when the androcentric outlook formed the basis for universal human rights, is silent in its articulations with regard to women. Over the course of time, and driven by the necessity to respond to the specific needs and challenges faced by women in forced displacement situations, refugee law and policy have evolved to ensure that gender-based persecution is included in the definition of the 1951 Convention.

The Convention on the Elimination of all forms of Discrimination Against Women (CEDAW) in 1979 recommended that state parties should interpret the definition of a refugee in the 1951 Convention in line with obligations of non-discrimination and equality. They should fully integrate a gender-sensitive approach while interpreting all legally recognised grounds for granting asylum, and classify gender-related claims on the ground of membership of a particular social group, where necessary.[5]

UNHCR has similarly stressed that the 1951 Convention requires a gender-sensitive interpretation that highlights "gender" as a relevant factor in the determination of refugee status claims. This approach takes into consideration the understanding that persecution is not necessarily or only caused by the person's gender but more so by the perpetrators' ideology, which dictates that people perceived to be deviating from their attributed gender role shall be persecuted, for example, the persecution of women perceived to be transgressing social norms. This approach by UNHCR is endorsed by a number of international bodies, including UNHCR's Executive Committee, which

> note(d) with appreciation special efforts by States to incorporate gender perspectives into asylum policies, regulations and practices; encourage[d] States, UNHCR and other concerned actors to promote wider acceptance, and inclusion in their protection criteria of the notion that persecution may be gender-related or effected through sexual violence; further encourage[d] UNHCR and other concerned actors to develop, promote, and implement guidelines, codes of conduct and training programmes on gender-related refugee issues, in order to support the mainstreaming of a

gender perspective and enhance accountability for the implementation of gender policies.[6]

UNHCR has long held the view that violence perpetrated by non-state actors against women, including gang and domestic violence, may constitute persecution in reference to asylum claims based upon membership in a particular social group. States with significant jurisprudence on refugee status determination such as Canada, the United Kingdom, Australia, New Zealand, and all EU countries have reached the same conclusion. Research conducted by UNHCR in Guatemala, Honduras, El Salvador, and Mexico highlights the pervasive and systemic levels of violence that women face, including gang and domestic violence, which forces them to flee. The women who were interviewed for the study emphasised that their sex compounded the difficulties they faced; this was particularly the case for transgender women.[7] In 2015, an inter-agency assessment report on the protection risks to women and girls in the European refugee and migrant crisis highlighted that women were fleeing countries of origin not just due to conflict but also in order to escape harmful gendered practices that impacted them and their daughters.[8] These experiences illustrate how gender discrimination contributes to forced displacement, and the need to identify and understand this as stemming from systemic and structural discrimination rooted in patriarchy.

Protection challenges faced by women and girls in forced displacement

Many of the protection challenges women and girls face in forced displacement situations are similar to the experiences of men and boys. However, there are specific gendered experiences of forced displacement that women and girls face. Toxic masculinities, internalised misogyny, and patriarchal societies, all contribute to structures that exclude and relegate women to a lower status than men. Widely accepted gender inequalities become further entrenched during displacement. Their tragic impact on women and girls is well known. It is this systemic inequality that also perpetuates the construct of women as the victim in a displacement discourse that legitimises their further exclusion and does not recognise and leverage their capacities or acknowledge their agency, even when most vulnerable.

The most visible manifestation of gender inequalities in displacement situations is the experience of gender-based violence (GBV) that women and girls face. While women, girls, boys, and men, all are at risk of GBV, this form of violence against women and girls is endemic. Humanitarian data shows that while approximately 35 per cent of women worldwide have experienced physical or sexual violence, this form of violence increases significantly in conflict settings. More than 70 per cent of women have experienced GBV in some crisis settings.[9] While these figures come from reported data, the untold story from unreported data could reveal much higher figures. Given how common experiences of GBV are for women and girls, responses to this are characterised by a "normalisation" of this experience vis-à-vis women and girls. This contributes to a dilution of not just outrage at these occurrences but also of the urgency to respond right from the start, including with the required GBV technical skills on the ground. Intimate partner violence, in particular, remains a massive challenge and requires a much greater understanding and recognition of power structures and relationships within which these violations occur, often with impunity. All of this points to the need for a much larger investment in and accountability towards strengthening comprehensive gender equality-related work that locates itself in developing awareness and education and actively enables communities to challenge gender inequalities.

These experiences are not unique to refugee populations. They also impact other population groups that UNHCR responds to, including internally displaced persons (IDPs), returnees, stateless persons, and those at risk of statelessness. Forcibly displaced women and girls face an increased risk of sexual and reproductive health and rights (SRHR) violations, with over 60 per cent of preventable maternal mortalities taking place in conflict, displacement, and natural disaster settings. There are also other negative effects arising from forced displacement that include an increase in girl child marriage, early and forced marriage, sexual slavery, economic losses stemming from the loss of livelihoods, and a loss of educational opportunities with the likelihood of adolescent girls being out of school increasing to 90 per cent in conflict zones when compared to girls in conflict-free countries.[10] The cumulative gendered impact of forced displacement is brutal on women and girls. In Syria, for example, the life expectancy of women is said to have declined from 75.9 years in 2010 to 55.7 years in 2014.[11]

Current humanitarian action places emphasis on increasing women's participation in decision-making processes that impact them. A recent report by UNHCR reveals how the focus on participation, without a comprehensive approach that takes into consideration the daily realities of internally displaced women, can unintentionally disempower women and girls in IDP situations and reinforce the dominance of men. For example, the over-reliance on consultation as a tool for engaging populations of concern has led to consultation fatigue amongst internally displaced women and girls and a lack of confidence on their part in humanitarian actors and governments to follow through on commitments and protect rights. Consultation processes can be disempowering when they do not result in a redistribution of power to women and girls. It is also unrealistic to aim for substantive and meaningful participation of women in IDP communities when humanitarian actors themselves struggle to model gender equality internally within their own agencies and governments.[12]

Nationality laws that do not grant women equality with men in conferring nationality to their children are a major cause of statelessness and a concern for UNHCR under its mandate to prevent and reduce statelessness. The adoption of the CEDAW led to a large number of states reforming laws that previously did not confer equal rights to women in nationality matters. Nonetheless, there still remain 25 countries in different parts of the world that have nationality laws that prevent equality between women and men relating to the conferral of nationality to children, thereby contributing to statelessness and the risk of it globally.[13]

For forcibly displaced women and returnees, a pressing lacuna is deeply linked with the capacity for self-reliance. This includes the need for decent work in order to support themselves and their families, securing housing, land and property rights, freedom from GBV, food security, education for themselves and their children, and a sustained process of healing and recovery, including for women and girl survivors of GBV. A 2011 consultation that UNHCR carried out globally with over a thousand forcibly displaced women in five regions highlighted their major concerns. These included access to individual documentation, participation, education, economic self-reliance, shelter, freedom from GBV and other forms of violence, health, access to sanitary materials, and support with legal issues as important areas that contribute to self-reliance.[14]

Strengthening strategies for change

A central focus area and indeed one of the most important strategies in addressing gender-related challenges is the meaningful participation of women and girls in decision-making and leadership processes. Participation is the process of redistribution of power; it is through this process that displaced and stateless women and girls can reclaim their personal and collective agency during the most difficult moments in their life.[15] UNHCR has institutionalised efforts to promote equal and meaningful participation of women, including through its Age, Gender and Diversity Policy (2018). The policy articulates a mandatory core action for all operations to ensure 50 per cent of female participants in management and leadership structures amongst populations of concern under UNHCR's authority and advocacy for the same with other partners, including governments.[16] The rigid power structures that keep women on the sidelines are very slow to change; moreover, courage and persistence are required to confront these inequalities in communities, the humanitarian system, and in national and local normative frameworks and institutions.[17] UNHCR operations have adopted several effective and context-specific strategies to enable women's participation and increase their influence in decision-making. These range from the establishment of women's committees in camps and urban areas across operations and strengthening women's representation in community elections through measures such as targeted trainings on leadership development, decision-making, communication and community-based awareness raising campaigns, and training on gender equality and women's rights.

These strategies have been combined with robust mechanisms to prevent, mitigate, and respond to GBV, including by providing support to known survivors; setting up referral pathways that allow access to medical, psychosocial, and legal services; and promoting inclusivity of services for all survivors, including men and boys, and individuals with diverse sexual orientation and gender identity. The Safe from the Start initiative that seeks to prevent and respond to GBV promotes multi-sectoral risk strategies and ensures that GBV prevention and response programme mainstreaming at the onset of emergencies includes the long-term goal of realising behavioural change to address the root causes of GBV.[18] This link between GBV prevention and response and comprehensive gender equality-related work needs to be strengthened further in order to sustain mainstreaming of GBV prevention efforts.

Complementary to the efforts to strengthen the protection of forcibly displaced persons, the detention of asylum seekers is subject to specific limits and safeguards in international law, as articulated and elaborated in UNHCR's Guidelines on Detention. These guidelines reflect the state of international law on detention for immigration-related purposes of asylum seekers. Specific considerations apply to the detention of asylum seekers with specific needs, including in particular victims of trauma or torture, children, and women. CEDAW recommends, as a general rule, that pregnant women and nursing mothers, who both have special needs, should not be detained. Where detention of women asylum seekers is unavoidable, separate facilities and materials are required to meet the specific hygiene needs of women. It further underlines the use of female guards and warders and that all staff assigned to work with women detainees should receive training relating to the gender-specific needs and human rights of women.[19]

To address the challenge of statelessness, the UNHCR launched the #IBelong Campaign to End Statelessness in 2014. The Campaign envisages the achievement of gender equality laws in all nations by the year 2024 as part of the campaign's broader goals and sets out a practical strategy through which this can be achieved in the Global Action Plan to End Statelessness.[20] Much progress has been made through this Campaign, including in 2017, with Madagascar and Sierra Leone becoming the first countries since the launch of the campaign to reform their nationality laws to allow mothers to confer their nationality to their children on an equal basis as men. Other countries also initiated discussions to reform their nationality laws, including Liberia and Eswatini who pledged in 2019 to resolve issues of gender discrimination in their respective nationality laws before the end of the #IBelong Campaign in 2024.[21] In Somalia, if enacted, a new draft Citizenship Bill will abolish discriminatory provisions and, inter alia, permit Somali women to confer nationality to their children on an equal basis as Somali men. The Parliaments of a number of other countries are currently examining proposals to review their respective nationality laws and are considering reforms that would allow women to confer citizenship to their children at birth.[22]

New ways of working: the Global Compact on Refugees

On December 17, 2018, 181 UN member states affirmed the Global Compact on Refugees (GCR). This was the result of 18 months of intensive consultation with member states and other stakeholders, including refugees themselves. The GCR sets out a blueprint for more timely, predictable, and comprehensive refugee responses. It builds on the foundations of the international refugee protection regime by providing an overarching framework for improved global sharing of burdens and responsibilities.

Global efforts to recognise and respond to refugee women and girls' specific needs and vulnerabilities have, in recent years, gained much traction at the policy level, as has the importance of gender equality. These principles are being translated into practice, albeit with differing levels of success, when it comes to improved participation and self-representation, registration, and other aspects of the humanitarian response. In the context of the GCR, refugee women themselves, alongside civil society actors and member states, repeatedly highlighted the importance of recognising the particular contributions that refugee women and girls can and are making, as well as the challenges that remain. The consultation process helped galvanise political will among both refugee hosting and donor countries to work towards real advancements across a range of different issues.

The GCR offers a number of opportunities for improving the situation for refugee women and girls worldwide. It seeks to set a standard in the manner in which age, gender, and diversity considerations, in particular with regard to refugee women and girls, are firmly integrated into the different arrangements and mechanisms that it sets out. Acknowledging existing barriers to women and girls' participation, empowerment, and leadership, the GCR seeks to highlight the various ways in which governments and other relevant actors could ensure refugee women and girls' safety, security, and meaningful engagement as important contributors to the social and economic life of a community.

The GCR further recognises the importance of gender equality as an overarching principle and the additional efforts that are required to ensure effective access to adequate health facilities and services, education, financial services, and the labour market.

As a global policy document, the GCR can help infuse national plans and efforts with a vision of gender equality mainstreamed across the various sectoral responses. It cannot, however, provide detailed guidance on how to overcome and move beyond existing cultural and political barriers at national and local levels regarding refugee women and girls' inclusion and participation. Rather, the GCR seeks to complement and enhance existing policy and protection frameworks, offering a tool that governments and stakeholders can use to advocate for and advance towards the progressive, systematic inclusion of refugee women and girls.

The first Global Refugee Forum (GRF), which was held in Geneva on December 17 and 18, 2019, offered an important opportunity for some of this goodwill and solidarity to be concretised. Envisaged as a follow-up mechanism to facilitate the implementation of the GCR, the GRF delivered over 1,400 pledges and contributions by various stakeholders, including member states, the private sector, UN agencies, non-governmental organisations (NGOs), and refugees. The pledges are informed by the four objectives of the GCR: easing the pressure on host countries, enhancing refugees' self-reliance, expanding access to third-country solutions, and improving conditions in the countries of origin. Pledges and contributions supported the various arrangements and mechanisms set out in the GCR (including the establishment of an Asylum Capacity Support Group) and focused on six cross-cutting themes, which include arrangements for international burden and responsibility sharing, education, jobs and livelihoods, energy and infrastructure, solutions, and protection capacity. There are specific gender considerations to each of these themes, and important stories to be told. A gender audit, commissioned by UNHCR, was conducted by refugee women and the University of New South Wales, Australia, throughout the GRF preparatory process – actively advocating with member states and other actors to ensure the inclusion of gender considerations in pledges and contributions. The forum offered an opportunity to showcase some of the good practices of refugee women and girls' entrepreneurship, advocacy and engagement, and build on these to ensure high-impact, focused contributions for refugee women and girls that would aim to shift the needle on gender and displacement-related issues over the coming years.

Conclusion

Listening to forcibly displaced women and girls, integrating their needs into response planning, and allocating adequate resources to implement this planning are the basic and logical steps required, without which the pursuit for gender equality would remain nothing more than tokenism. Forced displacement levels reached 79.5 million people worldwide at the end of 2019 as a result of persecution, conflict, violence, human rights violations or events seriously disturbing public order.[23] This calls for the need to focus on developing self-reliance for displaced persons in close collaboration with governments and through an approach that strengthens the humanitarian-development partnership and synergy. With approximately half of all displaced persons being women – in several contexts outnumbering men – there is an even greater need to focus on gender equality and translate the many global commitments made on gender equality, including on the Sustainable Development Goals, into reality.

The continued positive evolution of protection for refugees, and others of concern to the UNHCR, requires a true introspection on the barriers to progress on gender equality. Individual attitudes and structural obstacles, bolstered by these attitudes, perpetuate inequalities and contribute to the erosion of egalitarian values amongst individuals, communities, and nations. The 1994 Beijing Platform for Action acknowledges the principle of shared power and responsibility between men and women, as a matter of human rights and a condition for social justice. More than two decades later, some progress has been made, galvanised by the relentless struggles of women across the world, including forcibly displaced women. These struggles and victories must be met on our side with efforts focused on the transformation that seeks to support and enhance their rights and influence. This will require a more courageous and radical approach that endeavours to transform power relations and challenge the structural basis for gender inequalities.

Notes

1 This chapter reflects the position of UNHCR. UNHCR has not reviewed other contributions to this book, and the views expressed therein may not represent the views or position of UNHCR.
2 *Age, Race, Class and Sex: Women Redefining Difference in Sister Outsider Essays and Speeches* (Freedom, CA: Crossing Press 1984), pp. 114–123.
3 UN High Commissioner for Refugees (UNHCR), Handbook on Procedures and Criteria for Determining Refugee Status and Guidelines on International Protection Under the 1951 Convention and the 1967 Protocol Relating to the Status of Refugees, April 2019, HCR/1P/4/ENG/REV. 4, P9. Available at https://www.refworld.org/docid/5cb474b27.html (accessed Feb 7, 2020). It follows from the Preamble and Article 5 of the 1951 Convention that refugees should be accorded the widest possible exercise of their human rights and that the rights accorded to refugees through the 1951 Convention should not impair rights accorded to refugees through other instruments. The 1951 Convention is a dynamic instrument and should be read in the light of the full international human rights framework.
4 UN General Assembly, New York Declaration for Refugees and Migrants: resolution / adopted by the General Assembly, 3 October 2016, A/RES/71/1. Available at https ://www.refworld.org/docid/57ceb74a4.html (accessed Feb 7, 2020).
5 UN Committee on the Elimination of Discrimination Against Women (CEDAW), General recommendation No. 32 on the gender-related dimensions of refugee status, asylum, nationality and statelessness of women, 5 November 2014, CEDAW/C/GC/32. Para 38. Available at http://www.refworld.org/docid/54620fb54.html (accessed Feb 7, 2020).
6 UN High Commissioner for Refugees (UNHCR) 2000, Position paper on gender-related persecution. P1. Available at https://www.refworld.org/pdfid/3bd3f2b04.pdf (accessed Feb 7, 2020).
7 UN High Commissioner for Refugees (UNHCR) 2016, Women on the Run; First-hand account of refugees fleeing El Salvador, Guatemala, Honduras, and Mexico. P 15. Available at https://www.unhcr.org/publications/operations/5630f24c6/women-run.html (accessed Feb 7, 2020).
8 UNHCR, UNFPA, WRC 2015. Initial assessment report: Protection risks for women and girls in the European refugee and migrant crisis. Pp. 7–– Available at https://www.unhcr.org/569f8f419.pdf (accessed Feb 7, 2020).
9 Available at http://www.unwomen.org/en/what-we-do/humanitarian-action/facts-and-figures (accessed Feb 7, 2020).
10 Available at http://www.unwomen.org/en/what-we-do/humanitarian-action/facts-and-figures (accessed Feb 7, 2020).
11 Available at http://www.unwomen.org/en/what-we-do/humanitarian-action/facts-and-figures (accessed Feb 7, 2020).

Forced displacement

12 UN High Commissioner for Refugees (UNHCR) 2019, Tearing down the walls: Confronting the barriers to internally displaced women and girls' participation in humanitarian settings. Pp. 4—5. Available at https://www.unhcr.org/protection/women/5cd1a3394/tearing-walls-confronting-barriers-internally-displaced-women-girls-participation.html (accessed Feb 7, 2020).
13 UNHCR 2021, Background note on gender equality, nationality laws and statelessness, P 2. Available at https://www.refworld.org/docid/604257d34.html (accessed June 11, 2021).
14 UN High Commissioner for Refugees (UNHCR) 2011, Summary Report, Survivors, Protectors, Providers: Refugee women speak out. Available at https://www.unhcr.org/protection/women/4ec5337d9/protectors-providers-survivors-refugee-women-speak-summary-report.html (accessed Feb 7, 2020).
15 UN High Commissioner for Refugees (UNHCR) 2019, Tearing down the walls: Confronting the barriers to internally displaced women and girls' participation in humanitarian settings. P 55. Available at: https://www.unhcr.org/protection/women/5cd1a3394/tearing-walls-confronting-barriers-internally-displaced-women-girls-participation.html (accessed Feb 7, 2020).
16 UN High Commissioner for Refugees (UNHCR) 2018, Policy on Age, Gender and Diversity. Available at https://www.unhcr.org/protection/women/5aa13c0c7/policy-age-gender-diversity-accountability-2018.html (accessed Feb 7, 2020).
17 UN High Commissioner for Refugees (UNHCR) 2019, Tearing down the walls: Confronting the barriers to internally displaced women and girls' participation in humanitarian settings. P 55 Available at https://www.unhcr.org/protection/women/5cd1a3394/tearing-walls-confronting-barriers-internally-displaced-women-girls-participation.html (accessed Feb 7, 2020).
18 UN High Commissioner for Refugees (UNHCR), Safe from the Start Information Sheet. Available at https://www.unhcr.org/protection/women/53f31c819/safe-start-project-information-sheet.html (accessed Feb 7, 2020).
19 UN High Commissioner for Refugees (UNHCR), Submission by the Office of the United Nations High Commissioner for Refugees in the case of *R.R. and Others v. Hungary* (Application No. 36037/17) before the European Court of Human Rights, 3 November 2017. Available at http://swigea56.hcrnet.ch/refworld/docid/5a460ca04.html (accessed Feb 7, 2020).
20 Action 3 of the Global Action Plan to End Statelessness is to remove gender discrimination from nationality laws. Available at https://www.unhcr.org/protection/statelessness/54621bf49/global-action-plan-end-statelessness-2014-2024.html (accessed Feb 7, 2020).
21 UNHCR 2021, Background note on gender equality, nationality laws and statelessness, P 6. Available at https://www.refworld.org/docid/604257d34.html (accessed June 11, 2021).
22 UNHCR 2019, Global trends on forced displacement, P2. Available at https://www.unhcr.org/statistics/unhcrstats/5ee200e37/unhcr-global-trends-2019.html (accessed June 11, 2021).
23 Taken from https://www.unhcr.org/news/press/2014/6/53a42f6d9/resolve-conflicts-face-surge-life-long-refugees-worldwide-warns-unhcr-special.html (accessed Feb 7, 2020).

PART II
The path they travelled
Stories of refugee women

3
NARRATIVES OF REFUGEE WOMEN

Bernadette Vivuya, Laith Marouf, Rosy Fernando, Samia Zennadi, Sharmin Akther Shilpi, and Universal Just and Action Society

Refugee women are often doubly persecuted – they usually flee their homes to escape conflict and violence but suffer further violation of bodily integrity and loss of their political and socio-economic rights. Women and girls are more vulnerable to sexual violence, human trafficking, early and forced marriage, and material deprivation during displacement.

In addition to their precarious circumstances, they are excluded from decision-making processes within and outside of the household and the community. Their needs and demands continue to be ignored, which disenfranchises them even more.

This chapter, in contrast, presents narratives from women where they share their stories of grief, fortitude, and aspiration. These stories shed a light on the commonalities of experiences and issues faced by refugee women, in spite of their distinct circumstances cutting across class, ethnicities, religions, and regions.

Through their reflections, we get a glimpse into the protection and sustenance challenges faced by refugees, especially by women and children. We are also exposed to the intergenerational costs of denial of fundamental rights and essential services to refugees – such denial adds to the vulnerabilities and risks of exploitation for refugees, especially for women and girls, and entrenches the cycle of poverty and deprivation.

The narratives presented here are from Rohingya women who have fled Myanmar and are currently staying in refugee camps in Bangladesh's Cox's Bazar, Sri Lankan Tamil women who have been living in refugee camps in and on the outskirts of Chennai in India, Pakistani Hindu refugees in Rajasthan in India, Sahrawi women who have lived in asylum in Algeria almost all their lives, and women from Burundi, Rwanda, and Uganda who have found refuge in the Democratic Republic of Congo (DRC). We have also included stories of women

DOI: 10.4324/9781003047094-3

who have been internally displaced in Syria and of Bangladeshi women living in Cox's Bazar.

These stories were collected over a five-month period between September 2018 and January 2019. We have changed the names of some people in the stories to protect their privacy as per the request of the individuals.

Stories of Rohingya women in Bangladesh

Noor Bibi, 30 years

Noor Bibi arrived in Bangladesh in September 2017 with her husband and her five children. She has been living in Moinnarghona camp in Ukhiya, Cox's Bazar.

She recounts her escape from Myanmar vividly. She says that the members of the military and Maghs (Rakhine Buddhists) attacked their village at night. They started shooting rocket launchers and burning the houses. Noor and her family ran with others from the village to another locality nearby. She says that people had to carry their children and older relatives while fleeing.

Noor and her family stayed in this village for ten days. But soon the military arrived there as well and started destroying all the houses. By this time most of Noor's relatives had fled to Bangladesh. So, she and her husband gave all their gold to a local Arakanese man and paid him off to bring them to the border. From there they had to walk for five days to cross into Bangladesh. They would walk all day and take shelter at night. Then they would start their journey again the next morning, at the break of dawn.

Noor painfully recalls the persecution that she and others of her community had to face in Myanmar. She says that the military and other armed forces detained hundreds of people, slaughtered women and men, and killed their small children when the violence broke out in August 2017.

She says that even prior to this escalation in violence, they would face various forms of torture and harassment. There would be short periods of relative peace interspersed with regular harassment, and then bursts of violence.

Noor describes times when it was very difficult for people to even step out of their houses. They could not go to the bazaar or to their fields or other places of work. Her husband used to work as a stonemason in Myanmar. He would break and sell stones and also help in constructing roads to earn his living. But he would always be fearful of being detained by armed forces while working outside.

Noor elaborates on the targeting of Rohingya men by the police and the military. She says that they would arrest young men and torture them for information on Harakah al-Yaqin (now known as ARSA or Arakan Rohingya Salvation Army). They would accuse the men of being trained by ARSA and beat them up.

There were also cases of men from the armed forces abducting Rohingya women from the hospital or other public spaces such as roads. They would take the women back to their camps and torture them. Sometimes they would even kill the women, and their families would be left with nothing but speculation about their fate.

Noor says that the Maghs provoked and helped the military in torturing the Rohingyas. She explains that the Rohingyas were completely helpless. They could not resist because they were completely economically, socially, and politically disempowered.

The Maghs would take cows and goats that belonged to the Rohingyas. They would also take over the lands and properties of the Rohingyas and force them to work in their fields or in their homes instead. The Rohingya people would do work such as washing their clothes, helping in the repair and construction of their houses, etc. for meagre pay. Many times, they were not paid at all.

The Maghs would also threaten Rohingya women who worked in fields. At times they would also carry away the women and sexually assault and torture them.

As a result, the Rohingya women and girls would rarely step outside of their homes. It was, therefore, difficult for them to access schools or hospitals. Noor says that they would sometimes get medicines and birth control pills, etc. at a local hospital run by UNHCR, but mostly the women would go to their neighbourhood quacks.

There were also other challenges thrown up by the unsympathetic and discriminatory local administration. For example, Rohingya men and women would often have to pay local officers to register their weddings and get documents. The officers would demand amounts as high as 50,000 or 100,000 Bangladeshi takas, even though they know that the majority of the Rohingyas are living in poverty.

Noor expresses relief and gratitude about being in Bangladesh. She says that though they are unable to work, they are happy because they can sleep peacefully. They do not have to constantly worry or be afraid of being attacked by the Maghs or the military.

In the camp, the family survives on the rations and other items that they receive from aid agencies. They get rice and pulses twice a month. But Noor says that they often fall short of food and she is forced to borrow from others in the community.

Noor says that they are as comfortable as possible given the circumstances. But she also shares that one of the main problems that she has been facing on a daily basis is a lack of fuel for cooking. She cooks over a bark stove, but they are unable to collect lumber regularly and have to make do with the dry leaves and sticks that her husband gets from around the camp. During the rainy season, it becomes almost impossible for Noor to cook due to the unavailability of dry leaves.

She is happy that her children are able to study in the camp. She says that in Myanmar, it was impossible for girls to go to school, and even boys would have a very difficult time as all the teachers were Maghs and discriminated against the Rohingya students a lot.

Noor says that she would like to go back to Myanmar as that is her homeland. But she is vehement that their property, houses, domestic animals, etc. must be restored and returned. Moreover, the persistent persecution must cease, and the Myanmar government must guarantee that they would be protected, and their equal rights would be ensured, including the right to education and right to livelihoods.

Ayesha Begum, 28 years

Ayesha fled to Bangladesh at the beginning of September 2017, while she was four months pregnant. She says that the military and Maghs attacked her village. They raped and tortured the women and girls and killed them. Ayesha's mother was brutally beaten up. So they all ran to escape the violence.

She left alone with her children as her parents were reluctant to leave their home and she is estranged from her husband. They walked for two days until they reached the riverbank. She found a boatman and requested him to take them to Bangladesh but as they had no money to pay him with, he would not take them, and they were forced to stay put. After about 10–15 days, her parents found her there and they all crossed over after paying the boatman 40,000 takas.

Ayesha now stays in the camp with her children and her parents. She says that she is suffering a lot as her husband does not take care of their family. He has remarried and lives in the camp with his second family. Ayesha complains that her husband emotionally and mentally tortures her. She narrates that her husband took her elder son away from her without informing her. She looked for her son everywhere in desperation and found out that he was with his father. She begged and pleaded with him to let her take her son back, but he refused.

Yet Ayesha refuses to divorce him. She says that she wants him to provide shelter and food for the family, just as he does for his second family. She feels that it is impossible for her to look after her children as a single mother. She worries about how she would pay for their education and basic needs.

Ayesha regrets that she was unable to get an education in Myanmar because of the threat from the military. She says that one time some men claiming to be from the military came to their village and took away the girls who used to study, claiming that they would give them skills training. But they raped the girls and they became pregnant. After this incident, her father was too scared to send her to school. She says that if she had been literate, perhaps her husband would not have harassed her, and she would have found ways to be self-reliant.

Ayesha is now learning to sew at the women-friendly space in the camp.

Firoza Khatun, 30 years

Firoza was pregnant when she fled from Myanmar with her father, husband, and their children. They left their village when the military attacked and killed the Maulana and tortured two girls. Her in-laws were called for a village meeting, but they never returned. So Firoza and her husband decided to leave. They walked and reached Firoza's father's village where they stayed for a night. At night, they started hearing firing and explosions and ran deep into the forests. From there they made their way to the beach and crossed over to Bangladesh by boat.

It took them about four days to escape. Firoza says that the journey was extremely difficult for her as she ended up giving birth on the way and had to be on the move with her newly born baby. Moreover, they were constantly worried about being discovered or being stopped by the military. Their group was attacked by Maghs who wanted to rape a Rohingya girl travelling with them, but the group fought back and saved her. She heard of the armed forces attacking other girls and raping them and cutting open pregnant women's stomachs.

Firoza says that they were forced to flee in a hurry, and in those circumstances, they could not bring anything with them other than two pairs of clothes. She says that they had no intention of coming to Bangladesh and thought they would be returning to their village in a few days. But they soon realised that returning would be impossible and crossed the border.

On reaching Bangladesh, her father paid some money to a local Bangladeshi to allow them to build a house and stay on his land. They eventually started receiving ration and other utility items from aid agencies and now survive on them.

Firoza says that she would consider going back to Myanmar only if the government provides them access to basic services and facilities and gives them freedom. On being asked what freedom means to her, she says she would like to be able to move around as she wishes, without fear or hesitation.

Anowara, 15 years

Anowara came to Bangladesh in 2008 with her father, mother, and sisters. She says that her father had to come to Bangladesh for his medical treatment and was scared to leave his daughters back in Myanmar as they did not have a male sibling or guardian. So they all left Myanmar together and arrived in Teknaf.

Anowara says that her father used to catch and sell fish to sustain the family. But when his health deteriorated, Anowara and her elder sisters started doing odd jobs to support the household. They constantly shifted houses in Teknaf as people were reluctant to rent their houses to them. Then one local landlord hired them as guards and let them live on his property for five years.

Anowara and her family have now moved to the Rohingya camp in Teknaf. Two of her sisters are married to Bangladeshi men and live outside of the camp. She says that many Rohingya people have come and settled in Teknaf at different times over the years, but the authorities have mandated that people without a local birth certificate must return to the camp and stay there.

Anowara was very small when her family arrived in Bangladesh and she does not remember much about Myanmar. But her parents have told her about the torture and killings that were perpetrated by armed forces. She says that her cousin was accused of being a member of ARSA and killed by the military. They would also beat the men and women, burn their houses, and throw old people and children into fires.

Most of Anowara's remaining family members fled the latest outbreak of violence and are now living in Bangladesh. The few remaining aunts and uncles in Myanmar tell them on the phone to never return as things are still perilous and they are surviving with great difficulty.

Anowara says that she and her family do not wish to go back to Myanmar as they doubt that there will be ever-lasting peace. They feel that the violence will flare up again, leading to the torture and killing of the remaining Rohingyas. Her parents say that there is nothing left for them in Myanmar anymore, as they have heard from their relatives that their houses have been burnt to the ground, and their lands have been usurped.

Anowara says that others in the camp feel the same way. They say that they will not go back until the government returns their houses and properties to them and enables them to live peacefully and with dignity.

Majeda, 14 years

Majeda fled to Bangladesh with her siblings: five sisters and two brothers. Their parents were killed in Myanmar when the violence broke out. She and her siblings joined their neighbours when they left and walked for three days to cross the border.

Majeda talks about the everyday persecution that she and the others were subjected to. She says that Maghs would not allow people to work outside of their homes in peace or let the children go to school. They would steal cows and goats belonging to Rohingya people. If any Rohingya needed to go to the hospital for an emergency, they would have to risk harassment and pay off people at check posts, etc. to go to the town.

The Rohingyas feared stepping out, especially on the roads, as the Maghs would drive their cars over them. It was more dangerous for the women and girls to go out as they were always under threat of being kidnapped and raped, or killed. So, the girls would drop out of school and would largely be confined to their homes.

The men would usually work as farmers or fishworkers because they did not have access to any other jobs. But the fear of being targeted and attacked always loomed large. Majeda's father was killed while he was working in his field.

Majeda says they could not go to the mosque to pray; the military would fine them or torture them if they were discovered. They were afraid to even turn on the lights in their houses during Sehri (pre-dawn meal during Ramadan) as they could be targeted. They would have to hide and go to their relatives' houses on Eid and constantly be on the lookout for Maghs or military personnel.

In the camp, Majeda is glad for the sense of freedom and security that she feels. She and her family survive on the rice and pulses that they receive as aid. Sometimes, they sell a part of their rations to be able to buy other things.

She expresses the desire to be literate and self-reliant. She says that she has been learning to sew in Myanmar and now in the camp, and she would like to have her own sewing machine so that she can sustain herself.

Murshida, 13 years, and Samina

Murshida and her siblings came to Bangladesh after their mother and father were killed by armed forces. They lost one of their sisters in the violence. They escaped with their grandparents and are currently staying with their uncle and cousins.

Murshida remembers hearing guns being fired, and shortly thereafter their house was set on fire. Everyone started running in panic. When the military left their village, she and her siblings came back to the house and discovered the bodies of their parents and their sister. She thinks that they were shot and that the military men threw their bodies into the fire.

Murshida's father was the head Imam of their village and taught in the madrasa. He would sustain his family with the money he received from the mosque. Her mother worked in the house and cultivated vegetables, pepper, and paddy on her land.

Samina, Murshida's older cousin, says that as the Imam, her uncle faced a lot of difficulties in Myanmar. He was treated as an enemy by the local Maghs as he would teach Rohingya children.

Samina says that the government was wary of the Rohingyas becoming educated and aware, and so they starved them of any opportunity to study. The Rohingya children were not taught in any of the Burmese schools and the armed forces even targeted the Madrasas. There were a few Rohingya boys who were able to attain education till the higher grades after much struggle, but they would be afraid of teaching others lest they be persecuted for doing so.

Sometimes villagers would pool their resources together and find Muslim teachers willing to teach their children, but it had to be done in complete secrecy. It was thus not a sustainable system and the children were able to learn very little.

Samina says that it was especially difficult for girls to receive education. She says that the girls were not allowed to go to school or step out of their houses as people were afraid that they would be teased or worse, taken away by the Maghs.

She also says that most Rohingyas considered it to be pointless to risk their lives for the little education that they received, as there were no jobs available to them. The Rohingyas were not allowed to go out from their villages and were forced to survive on farming and related activities. She states that there were no benefits to studying, as there were no sources of income.

Samina says that the government did not allow any NGOs to function directly in Rakhine. When the NGOs would apply for permissions to operate, the government would sign contracts with them taking the responsibility of utilising the funding. Samina has heard that a huge percentage of this amount would be embezzled and whatever remained would be used for its intended purpose.

Samina shares that she faced a lot of trouble in getting her daughter married. The local authorities demanded 100,000 takas to give them the legal documents recognising the marriage. They would charge exorbitant amounts as they pleased from the families.

One of their cousins used to drive CNG delivery vehicles for a living. Samina says that they would often be stopped at check posts and if they were found carrying fuel or other such utility items from one village to another, they were charged a fee of up to 10,000 takas to be let through.

She says the Rohingya people are perpetually sick. They had to toil hard day and night to sustain themselves, and still they could not manage enough food or healthcare. The Maghs would take away their cattle and other precious items. They would even loot them of their gold ornaments and money.

Samina says that most girls were forced to spend all their time indoors doing household chores, learning Arabic to read the Quran, or teaching each other how to sew. They would also cook and take care of their parents.

Samina expresses regret and sadness about having been born in Myanmar. She reflects upon the degrading treatment that the Rohingyas had to put up with and says that she does not want to go back to Myanmar. She says that if the Bangladesh government were to send them back, the international community would first have to ensure that the Myanmar government legally recognises them as Rohingya and as citizens of Myanmar and gives them equal rights.

Nurunnahar, 30 years

Nurunnahar and her family lives in Moinar Ghona. She originally came from Myanmar as a refugee several years ago but has since been assimilated with the local Bangladeshi community.

She shares the myriad ways in which the new Rohingya arrivals have impacted her life. She says that her husband used to cultivate vegetables in their field and sell them for a living earlier, but he is currently unemployed as their field has been taken over to build an orphanage for Rohingya children.

When they lost the land, her husband started cultivating spinach in the canal and selling it. But one of the local NGOs built a garbage dump next to the canal, from where sewage seeps into the water, making it impossible for them to grow spinach. Thus, cut off from their only sources of income, Nurunnahar and her family survive on the meagre income of her eldest son, who is a mason.

Nurunnahar is wary of complaining about her land to the authorities; she is shy and does not want any trouble, and it was disputed land, to begin with, as her husband's brothers have filed cases claiming ownership over it.

She says that the refugees and host community members existed in harmony earlier. But due to the sheer number of people who have moved into the community in a very short period of time, the lives of the locals have been thrown into disarray.

The commodity prices in the local bazaar have increased a lot and people like Nurunnahar who are unable to cultivate any longer are forced to spend more on food products and other utilities. Moreover, the trees on the surrounding hills have been cut to accommodate the growing numbers of refugees. Nurunnahar used to practice horticulture and grow betel nut and other fruits which she cannot do anymore because the trees have been cut down. She says that other locals are facing similar conditions, where their expenses have gone up, but the sources of livelihoods are diminishing.

Nurunnahar exclaims that she cannot do anything but accept her fate. She says that she hopes that the Rohingya people would not continue living there forever in the existing conditions, as it would be unsustainable. But she adds that she does not want the government to drive them away because they have nowhere to go. She wishes for a peaceful and sustainable resolution.

She says that in case the refugees are unable to go back, they will all find a way to live together somehow. Nurunnahar is living among the refugees on a hill inside the camp. She cooks for them when she can and provides them with water to bathe and for other purposes. She says that the Rohingyas have already suffered a lot and are helpless. She feels sad for them and wants to help as much as she can. Some of them even come into her yard and rest there. She says that she considers them to be her family members and they in turn treat her as they would treat their mothers.

Rahima, 36 years

Rahima and her family escaped to Bangladesh in 1992. She says that the military and other armed forces used to forcefully detain people for days at a stretch and torture them or kill them. Some men from the military came to their house one day and took her father away. They had no news of him for seven days. When he came back, they found out that he had been tortured in custody. He decided that it was not safe for his family to live in Myanmar anymore and they left.

There were other factors that forced them to flee as well. Rahima says that they could not keep any poultry or cattle to sustain themselves, as the Maghs would come and steal them. They even entered people's houses to loot them and take away their food grains, etc. When people protested, the Maghs would say that Myanmar is not a country for Rohingyas and that they should leave.

Rahima and her family travelled to Bangladesh by boat. They reached Shah Porir island and then made their way to Teknaf. She says that initially they stayed in different people's houses, a couple of days at a time. They had not brought anything with them except two pans, a few clothes, and some money. After a few days, they cleared up part of a hill and set up a shelter there. They did not have access to any drinking water, bathrooms, or latrines. Whatever little money they had, they spent it on buying food. She remembers that the first week was extremely difficult. But after seven days, they were able to get themselves registered as refugees and started getting ration.

Rahima says that she does not remember much from that time as she was very young, but her parents had to suffer a lot. She says that things have improved, and their quality of life has become better. They have been provided with a food card worth 700 takas and they can buy rations and utilities using this money. Besides, they receive basic food items such as rice and lentils in aid.

She shares that it is also possible for men and women to work inside the camp and earn some money. She says that the women cultivate and sell vegetables, rear chickens, and sew clothes and nets, etc. They are also allowed to work as sewing trainers in the women-friendly spaces, for which they are paid about 3,500 takas per month.

But most of the work is either voluntary or pays very little as the refugees are not allowed to sell any products outside of the camp. For example, the sanitary napkins that some of the women make are not meant for sale but for distribution among refugee women. Other items that the residents, both men and women, make include utility items such as toothpastes and soaps.

The men also run grocery shops, mobile repair shops, etc. within the camps. Rahima says that a few of them work in the surrounding area of the camp, but they are not allowed to go outside without permission.

She recalls that back in Myanmar, her father used to work in the fields and sell fish, while her mother worked at home, as women did not work outside the house generally. She says that earlier it was not uncommon for Rohingya children to go to school and for the men who finished their education to become teachers.

But she has heard from her relatives who escaped and came to Bangladesh in 2017 that the situation has massively deteriorated and that their houses and land have been destroyed.

Rahima says that she wants to live in peace, be it in Bangladesh or another country. She says that if they must be sent back to Myanmar, their safety has to be ensured first. Otherwise, the Bangladesh government or humanitarian agencies must arrange for them to be settled in another country where they can live without violence and fear.

Rahima claims that she wants freedom. She does not want to be constricted from moving outside of her house and to feel scared that her house and her belongings would be taken away from her. She wants to be able to educate her children and ensure that they have bright futures.

Her daughters and son are currently studying in schools inside the camp and are learning both Bangla and English. Rahima says that when they were in Myanmar, she and her family did not realise the value of education as they faced so many other immediate threats and challenges. But after having lived in Bangladesh for so long, she considers it very important to be literate and to be able to get decent jobs to lead a good life.

Roshida Begum, between 40 and 45 years

Roshida Begum arrived in Bangladesh in September 2017. She has studied till grade 2 but cannot be sure of her age. She says that she and her family crossed into Bangladesh along with hundreds of people six days after Eid-Ul-Adha. They left Myanmar by boat and reached Shah Porir island, where they stayed in a mosque for a night. The Imams from the mosque brought them to the Thengkhali camp in a car.

She says that they had to pay the boatmen up to 100,000 Burmese Kyat per person. Since Roshida did not have any money, she gave the boatman all her gold. Thereafter, they had no money to spend on food or other essential items, but she says that the Imams provided them food, medicines, and first aid along the way.

Upon reaching Thengkhali, local Imams approached them and gave them canvases for shelter and essential items such as dry ration, pots and pans, rice, potatoes, oil, toothbrushes, soaps, and even some money. Roshida and her family bought bamboo and found a spot on the hillside to set up their tent. She says that she and her children were homeless for almost 12–13 days because they could not find a clear space to set up their tent among the thousands and thousands of families.

Roshida narrates that the situation in Myanmar had worsened over the last six years. She says that there was peace before that, albeit fraught, but for the past six years it has been nothing but sorrow. The Rohingyas could not sleep as disturbing thoughts about whether the military was coming to attack them and whether they would get beaten up or shot would keep going through their minds.

She describes various forms of torture that the Rohingya people had to bear on a daily basis. Their girls were taken away, never to return, and the boys and men were brutally beaten up. The Maghs would attack Rohingya people when they were outside, on their way to work, or to the market. They would beat them and rob them. Roshida was also beaten up on her way to work a few times. They would also enter Rohingya houses and take away all their valuables.

The children could not go to school in this environment of fear. It was also almost impossible for Rohingya people to go to hospitals or to the towns, and there was a pervasive fear that if they went to a local hospital, they would be killed. Roshida says that she lost one of her daughters at childbirth because she could not go to a hospital.

In the days leading up to the exodus of the Rohingyas, Roshida describes horrifying scenes of how the armed forces and Maghs started attacking women and girls. They were raped, their hands were chopped off, and their breasts were cut off. Sometimes their throats were slit and they would be left for dead.

She says that she and her family fled with a large group of people. Along the way, they saw entire villages emptied and burnt. While they were crossing the river, many people died as few overloaded boats capsized.

Roshida laments that she never wanted to leave Myanmar, but they had had enough of the torture and killings. The military killed her 18-year-old son and threw his body into the river. Roshida looked for his body for three days but could not find it. She says that she and the others crossed over into Bangladesh because they knew that the military or Maghs could not harm them there. She says that she is thankful that they have a roof over their heads and food to get by. But, most importantly, she is grateful that they are able to sleep again.

Roshida shares that one of the major challenges she faces is to ensure a decent life for her children. Being a single mother to small children (her husband lives separately with his second wife and their family), she does not have a source of income or support. Though they have enough food so as not to starve, she would like an avenue to earn some extra money to buy other utilities and supplies.

Roshida and the others want justice. They want the Myanmar government to recognise them as equal citizens so that they can fearlessly go back to their country. They do not want to live like second-class citizens anymore and want equal status for all religions in Myanmar.

Roshida says that she would consider going back to Myanmar only if there is an internationally recognised and enforceable agreement which guarantees their safety in Myanmar. She also says that the humanitarian and international agencies such as the UN must ensure their protection and well-being in Myanmar as they would not be able to build their lives back up and survive otherwise. She ends on a grim note saying that just because she and her family managed to escape and come to Bangladesh after the most recent spate of violence does not mean that they would survive another one if sent back.

Khurshida, 35 years; Laila Begum, 28 years; and Ayesha, 31 years

Khurshida, Laila Begum, and Ayesha are from Ukhiya, Cox's Bazar in Bangladesh. Their lives have been significantly transformed since the Rohingyas started coming into Bangladesh in large numbers in August 2017. As women from the host communities, all aspects of their lives be it their livelihoods, wages, access to basic services, and commodities have been impacted.

They say that some of the women used to collect and sell leaves and sticks from the hills to earn their living. Some of the other women either worked at other people's homes or were engaged in farming.

But since the forests were cleared to accommodate the growing refugee population, the women have been unable to collect fruits, firewood, etc. Moreover, the lands that they cultivated have been converted into camps for the refugees as well, depriving them of their source of income.

The women say that since their incomes have shrunk, it has been difficult for them to send their children to school regularly or to even manage more than a meal a day sometimes.

They say that the Rohingyas are cordial and that the women do not feel unsafe despite so many unknown people having moved into their neighbourhood. One of the women recalls that there was an episode where a few Rohingya youths tried to tease a local woman, but they desisted after a warning and nothing like that has happened since. In fact, the elderly Rohingyas look out for the girls and women from the host Bangladeshi community.

The women share that they have been pushed deeper into poverty. They and their husbands do not get work due to increased competition in the labour market. They say that the work that they would do for 200 takas earlier is now being done by Rohingyas in as little as five takas, and therefore, they get hired more easily.

On the other hand, the prices of commodities have increased after the arrival of the refugees. The women from the host community struggle to buy things for their daily use.

They also talk about the challenges of sanitation. The camps and existing settlements are so closely cramped together that the hygiene levels are extremely low. The women share that their poultry such as hens and ducks have been dying off by ingesting the garbage strewn around. They also share that they used to bathe in the nearby pond earlier because they do not get tapped water in their houses, but now the water in the pond has become extremely polluted and they cannot use it for anything. They also struggle with access to latrines, which were built to be shared communally but have become unusable due to the increased number of people.

The women have no choice but to mourn the loss of the cultivable lands and forests and other services. They do not know who to approach with their complaints. In any case, they wonder who would listen to them. They say that the well-off families have not been adversely affected by the huge in-migration, but it is the poor who are forced to endure hardships.

They express that they do not want the Rohingyas to be forcibly sent back. Instead, they feel that both the Bangladeshis and the Rohingyas would be able to live in peace and harmony with each other until Myanmar allows the Rohingyas back into their land. But they wish that the government and NGOs would do more to help and support the local community.

Stories from Sri Lankan Tamil women in India

Padma Jothi, 45 years

Padma Jothi is from Mullaitivu and has lived in India for the past 28 years. She is married with two children. She initially lived in the Namakkal-Paramathi camp and moved to Gummidipoondi SLR camp in Chennai, Tamil Nadu, after marriage. Her husband is a painter by profession. Padma Jothi studied till 9th grade in Sri Lanka but had to abandon her studies when they came to India as the family did not have the means to educate her.

Padma Jothi's parents were farmers in Sri Lanka, and they owned a house and agricultural land. She grew up with seven siblings, four brothers and three sisters.

She talks about how difficult it was to live through the war. There were non-stop bombings and shootings, and people lived in constant fear of being killed. She remembers that the family was forced to live in an underground bunker and eat by candlelight. There was also an acute scarcity of food as normal lives were disrupted and they could not farm or buy anything. She vividly recalls how she and her family could not sleep for days on end and often had to run from the village into the forest to hide. Tired of feeling terrorised and desperate all the time, her father finally decided to escape to India.

They left Mullaitivu and went to Mannar from where they took a boat to India. Padma Jothi says that they had to pay the boatman a fee of SLR 5,000 each. Throughout the journey on foot and by boat, the family was fearful of being killed in the crossfire or being discovered by the army or the navy.

Luckily, they all made it to Dhanushkodi and went to the local police station to register as refugees. Padma Jothi remembers that they were received cordially by the Indian authorities. The refugees were vaccinated and then readied for travel to Coimbatore by bus. But on reaching Coimbatore, the authorities discovered that they could not accommodate all the families in the camp there, and the refugees were then taken to Namakkal-Paramathi Camp. Along the route, the authorities took good care of the people and provided them with food and water.

Once Padma Jothi and the others reached the Paramathi camp, they were given photo IDs and allowances. She says that at the time, the allowance was INR 75 for male refugees, INR 60 for female refugees, and INR 30 for children. The refugees were also given 6 kg of rice, 500 g sugar, and 3 L of kerosene. Each of the families was allotted a shack with a thatched roof, among rows of such shelters.

The allowances have since been increased, and male refugees now receive INR 1,000 and female refugees receive INR 750. The families also receive INR 400 for each child. However, the total amount is meagre and does not allow families like Padma Jothi's to meet their needs. Most people in the camp therefore work in the informal sector to supplement their incomes. But due to their extremely low wages, they live hand-to-mouth, even having to go hungry at times.

Padma Jothi says that people in the camps have no complaints as far as the local authorities are concerned, who come once a month to conduct an inspection and mark the attendance of the refugees in registers. The refugees are satisfied that they are able to educate their children. Padma Jothi says that she sends her two sons to private school, and though the school is expensive, they get substantial concession as the children are good at studies.

The most pressing issue for the people remains that of getting gainful employment. Padma Jothi narrates that the boys and girls from the camp are unable to get decent, well-paying jobs despite their good schooling and college degrees. They often have to settle for odd jobs with poor wages. Many of them are working as painters and drivers as those are the only jobs available to them. She says that the youths in the camp are frustrated and often dejected. They are very stressed all the time, making it hard for the parents to console them.

Sometimes the boys might do something wayward out of their frustration and they get picked up by the authorities. When their parents go to get them released, they are abused and insulted by the police. Padma Jothi says that people take the abuse and humiliation without protest, despite being from respectable families. She says that there are no threats to their safety, but not so much when it comes to their dignity.

Padma Jothi has been trained in tailoring. She says that she stitches nighties, blouses, trousers, etc. But she cannot work outside the camp, so she has to make do with whatever little work she gets inside the camp. She is also a member of a self-help group (SHG). It has 12 other members, and they save INR 200 a month and deposit INR 10 to the SHG per month. They have registered an account and even took out a loan of INR 60,000, which they used to meet expenses related to school fees, repayment of small loans, and other household needs.

In some of the families, the men have been able to go abroad, and they send money to their parents for maintenance. Similarly, some of the girls are married to boys who live abroad and help their families. But generally, life is quite difficult for most people, and their troubles are tied to the lack of livelihoods.

The conditions of the camp are also quite poor. It is low-lying, and the roads are not laid properly. The drains are not covered, and during the rainy season, the water flows onto the road and becomes stagnated. There is frequent flooding in the camp. The camp residents have made representations for covering the drains and laying the roads, but nothing has been done for almost three years. She says that sometimes when a roof collapses or other severe damage happens to a house, then the authorities give them INR 3,000 for repairs and maintenance. But that amount is rarely given out and it is not enough anyway.

Despite the challenges, Padma Jothi says that they feel scared at the prospect of repatriation. They feel that they would have to start from scratch and rebuild their lives. Although the government provides INR 10,000 to returnees, there is no employment available to them. Their lands and houses are long gone, and people are doubtful if they will be able to get land when they go back. Due to these doubts, they feel that they are better off living here and coping with the conditions, rather than throwing their lives into a spin again.

Moreover, the younger generation is even more resistant to the idea of going back. They were born and have grown up in India. They do not know anything about Sri Lanka and do not think of it as their homeland.

They have witnessed the cases of a couple of families from the camp that went back to Sri Lanka but have now returned due to the lack of livelihoods. But upon return, these families were not allowed to live in the camps as they lost their refugee status. Their other allowances were stopped too. Now, they have to live with their relatives in conditions even worse than before.

So Padma Jothi says that given the choice, it is likely that most of them would like to stay in India. She does not know if this would be the right decision, but she is certain that it would be better than upheaving their lives again.

She says that sometimes she feels extremely wretched and distraught; she thinks that it is their fate to live poor, uncared for, and without dignity and respect. But at other times, she feels grateful that at least she and her children are able to live freely and sleep peacefully. She continues to hope that their lives will change for the better, and they will live with equal opportunities and respect as Indian citizens.

Jayapriya, 30 years

Jayapriya was born in Vavuniya, Sri Lanka, in 1988. She came to India with her parents as a 2-year-old. Her family was engaged in farming back in Vavuniya, but the civil war made it impossible for them to carry on with agriculture and make a living. As the situation became more difficult and dangerous, her father decided to take the risk of fleeing and coming to India with his family. So Jayapriya, along with her parents and her three siblings, came to India.

Her family travelled with a few other families to Dhanushkodi, Tamil Nadu, by boat. She does not recall anything about the journey, but her parents have mentioned to her that crossing the rough sea was extremely dangerous and risky.

She says that the police registered them at Dhanushkodi and brought the entire group to the Gummidipundi SLR camp. Jayapriya has lived there since and remembers nothing about her life in Sri Lanka. She says that their lives in India have been full of ups and downs, especially for her parents, who left everything behind and struggled hard in an alien country to rebuild their lives as refugees on the basis of whatever little support they received.

Jayapriya says that their lives here are peaceful but laments that there is no justice for them. The entire community has suffered a lot because of the war and the displacement, and the constant fear, timidity, helplessness, and uncertainty has exacted a huge physical and emotional cost from the people. Jayapriya gets despondent at this point and wonders aloud why she, her family, and close ones had to suffer in this manner.

She gathers herself and starts talking about her family. She had an arranged marriage with a man from the same camp, and they now have two children, a girl and a boy. Her husband's family is also from Vavuniya. He has studied till 10th grade and works as a truck driver. Jayapriya has studied till 12th grade and works as a homemaker. She says that it is difficult to find a decent job as a refugee, and the women and girls usually get paid very little, which is not enough to meet their needs.

Her husband has a regular income, but the money he brings is just about enough to manage the basic expenses of their family. Jayapriya is concerned about future expenses and whether they would be able to meet the education and health-related costs for their children as they grow up. She says that they have been getting the same allowance and entitlements for years, but in the meantime the expenditure on education has been increasing.

Adding to her frustration is the fact that youngsters with good education are unable to get decent jobs which are appropriate to their qualification and skills. She says that the parents work hard to save money and sacrifice whatever they can to give their kids a good education, but it is not enough to ensure that they would have good jobs and decent lives.

She also talks about the constant baggage of being a refugee. Although the community members have never faced any problems from the local host community, they have been unable to integrate or assimilate with them. Jayapriya feels that they are "othered" and treated as refugees wherever they go. The lives of refugees are always full of struggles and uncertainties, and with little hope, she says. She wishes for an easier and peaceful life with dignity and justice.

She says that she often discusses the possibility of going back to Sri Lanka with her friends in the camp. The elder members in the camp often speak about their lives and the possessions that they left behind in Sri Lanka. But the younger generation like Jayapriya is troubled by the uncertainty and the potential lack of prospects in Sri Lanka. They are concerned whether they would get adequate assistance or decent livelihoods to help rebuild their lives there.

Jayapriya is, therefore, extremely conflicted. On the one hand, she came to India when she was merely 2 years old, and she feels like India is her country. On the other hand, she has an acute sense of the fact that she is an outsider here, a refugee, and hence must go back some day.

She narrates that her husband did go back to Sri Lanka for a short while. The family did not join him as they were not sure whether it would be safe to go back. Her husband was able to find a house and a job there and asked Jayapriya and the children to join him. But they refused to move at the time because all their family members and friends were in the camp.

Jayapriya feels that her and her children's future is in India and that somehow they will overcome their day-to-day challenges and make a better life for themselves. She asked her husband to come back, and he went back to his old job, working hard and saving enough to get his children a good education. Jayapriya hopes that this decision was the right one and that it would allow them to have happier and better lives, in this country that is now home to them.

Ramana Devi, 47 years

Ramana Devi was born in Karavatti, Jaffna, in 1971 and is the fourth among seven siblings. She came to India in 2006 when she was about 35 years old.

She tears up as she recounts the massive toll that the war has exacted on her family. Her father, Mr. Kandasami, a cooperative union driver, died in the war when he was just 50 years of age. Another close relative, Selva Rathnam, was heavily wounded during the war and died of his injuries in a hospital.

In 1990, she got married to Sri Guhan, and her son Umeshan was born in September 1991. In 1992, her husband went missing in the war and his whereabouts are not known to this date. The family is unaware whether he is alive or dead.

Ramana Devi, who has studied till 11th grade, reflects on her life in Karavatti and says that her family were landowners and were largely engaged in farming. They grew all their food, including cereals, pulses, and vegetables, and owned a tractor to plough the fields. Ramana Devi recalls an incident where the cadre members of the LTTE came to their field and forcefully took the tractor from them. She also talks about the death of one of her brothers at the hands of the Sri Lankan Army. He was shot dead at the young age of 16.

The family thus lived with the ever-present threat of violence and were caught in the crossfire between the LTTE and the Sri Lankan army, like many other civilian families. Their simple and self-sufficient lives were disrupted by the constant difficulties and dangers that the war threw up, and one by one, Ramana Devi's siblings started leaving Sri Lanka. They all fled to different countries after having paid lakhs of rupees to agencies to facilitate their travel. She says that all her siblings are now living either in France or England and are well-settled with families.

Ramana Devi talks about the days leading up to her flight from Sri Lanka. She says that as the Sinhala army made their way up to her village sometime in 2005, she along with several others from her village fled to Paruthi Thurai in Jaffna. She and her family went to a friend's house where she met with other people who were on the run. They all left for Kattupirai, Jaffna, and from there reached Trincomallee by ship. Thereafter, they took a bus up to Colombo where they stayed in a rented house for four months. The rent of the house was SLR 10,000 a month.

She then came to India on a tourist visa after obtaining her passport and visa in Colombo. She went straight to Madipakkam, to her brother-in-law's place, and stayed there for three months. In the meantime, she went to Rameshwaram Camp with her son and they both registered themselves as refugees.

Her son now lives with his family in Gummidipundi SLR camp, with other families from different parts of Sri Lanka, particularly from Mannar and Vavuniya. He is married and has a 2-year-old daughter. There are approximately 3,500 families at the camp. They all have different forms of identification, including ID cards, ration cards, and Aadhar cards (which serve as individual identity proofs). The Indian government provides the families with allowances, totalling around INR 4,700 per month. The refugees in the camp are also entitled to secondary hospital care and rations (the entitlements per family include 20 kg of free rice, 10 kg of rice at a reduced price, and pulses and oils, including kerosene).

But Ramana Devi does not stay in the camp due to ill health. She continues to live in Madipakkam and supports herself through her income of INR 12,000 per month.

When asked about her desire to go back to Sri Lanka, Ramana Devi becomes pensive. She says that she wants to go back to her country, but her sisters have advised her not to. Her son and his wife do not want to go back either as they are wary of the uncertainty it would lead to and concerned about what life in post-war Sri Lanka would entail. She thinks that she and her family have a peaceful life here in India, and things would be much more difficult for them in Sri Lanka. She does admit that they face degrading situations at times, especially from authorities, for example if the boys from the community are hauled up for any wrongdoing or transgressions, the entire community is targeted. The officials sometimes act as if they do not know what "mercy" is, she says.

Ramana Devi says that it is unlikely that things will change in her lifetime, unless they take the daunting decision of going back to Sri Lanka. In the meantime, they can only hope for the best, both for the elders and for the children of the camp. Their hopes are intimately tied up with good education for the youth, which they think would allow them to access good jobs and have reasonable incomes and comfortable lives. She ends with a reflection about whether there will ever be a "good life" for her, and the thousands of other families in the camps.

Jensy Niraja, 34 years

Jensy was born in Trincomallee, Sri Lanka, in 1985. She came to India in 1990 as a 5-year-old with her parents and her two elder siblings, a brother and a sister. She recalls that they travelled in a large group with several other families and that they arrived at Mandapam from where all of them were taken to Pollachi camp, Tamil Nadu.

As a child, Jensy did not spend much time in the camp as she was enrolled in the government hostel in Tirunelveli and completed her secondary education there. She remembers her hostel life as being full of difficulties and problems, as she always felt that she was at the mercy of the school authorities. She kept to herself and focussed on studying, with occasional visits from her parents.

Jensy returned to the Pollachi camp to live with her parents after completing her schooling. She later got married to a man from the Gummidipundi SLR camp and moved there to live with him and his family. She now has two sons, one in the 4th grade and another who is 2 years old.

She says that her family fled to India to escape the atrocities of the war and from the Sri Lankan Army. When asked about her journey to India, she says that all she remembers was the ordeal of getting to India. She remembers that everyone was in a constant state of fear of being discovered by the army and hence kept running and hiding in the forests to escape detection.

Growing up in India, Jensy has forgotten most of what her life was like back in Sri Lanka. All she knows about Sri Lanka now is what she has heard from her parents and from others in the camp and at school.

She says that her life in India has had its fair share of problems, but they have learnt not to complain as they get to live on and that is what matters most. She elaborates that the treatment meted out to them by government authorities is at times bothersome but is quick to add that they have become used to these occasional irritants and soon forget them.

Jensy is grateful for the employment opportunities available to the refugees, although they are too few and mostly accessible only to men. The men of the camp work as daily-wage labourers, painters, delivery personnel, and drivers. They usually earn INR 5,000–10,000 per month and have to work anywhere around 9 to 12 hours a day.

The women and girls at the camp remain largely homebound. A majority of them are homemakers, but a few of them do odd jobs in supermarkets or shopping malls in order to support their families.

Jensy expresses regret that the girls and boys of the community cannot get better jobs, despite being well-educated. She says that young people in the camp have worked hard to become engineers, doctors, nurses, physiotherapists, etc. but are not considered for government jobs due to their status of being refugees and are unable to access jobs in the private sector. The women are especially disadvantaged, as they might be skilled or qualified to work as tailors or nurses but are usually confined to working as domestic workers. This lack of jobs and self-sufficiency remains the major cause of sadness and worry amongst the people in the camp, as they would like to ensure better futures for their children.

Jensy shares her own ideas on how the lives of the people at the camp could be improved. She talks about the inadequacy of the support that they receive. She says that in spite of the prices of food grains and other essential commodities spiralling upwards, their allowances remain the same. She wishes that the allowance would be revised so that they are able to ensure three good meals and a decent education for their children.

Jensy also draws attention to the quality of accommodation in the camp. The community members live in small, thatched houses. People have made additions to the original structure to make them more comfortable, but they are not enough to protect them from inclement weather. She says that the thatched roofs leak when there are rains, and the entire camp gets completely flooded as it is in a low-lying area and there is no drainage system.

She also talks about the lack of safety inside and outside the camp, which makes it extremely difficult for the women and girls to move around. Alcoholism is rampant in the camp, and the women are fearful of being harassed by drunk men.

Given the difficulties that women face in finding jobs outside the camp, Jensy says that they would be interested in self-help initiatives such as candle-making, incense-making, and tailoring. In fact, many of the women are trained in tailoring and can sew a variety of dresses. But due to the lack of access to support services such as credit and markets, they are unable to pursue any profession and make a living.

Jensy hopes to get Indian citizenship one day, as that seems to be the only way for her to ensure good education for her children and to enable them to get decent jobs. She says that she has not thought about repatriation at all, as she does not know much about Sri Lanka and considers India to be her home. When she hears other people in the camp longing to go back to Sri Lanka, she is unable to relate to them as India is the only country that she knows and has felt at home in.

But her identity as a refugee seems to have rendered Jensy stateless in her mind. She is not truly Sri Lankan anymore, and not Indian yet either.

Rohini, 49 years

Rohini was born in 1969 and arrived in India in 1990 at the age of 18. Her father was a veterinary doctor in Mannar, and she has five siblings, three sisters and two brothers.

Currently she resides in the Gummidipoondi SLR Camp. She has studied only till 9th grade as she could not afford to continue her studies in India. She got married to a man from the same camp in 1994. Her husband has studied only till the 6th grade and works as a daily-wage labourer.

Rohini's journey to India was similar to many others in the camp from Mannar. She and her family escaped in a boat, avoiding the Sri Lankan army and navy. They paid SLR 3,000 per head for the trip and reached Dhanushkodi in India. She remembers that they had to walk for many miles along the seashore to reach the boat. She recalls that as soon as they got into the boat, some of the people fainted due to tension and exhaustion. Her sister, who had a new-born baby of only 40 days old, was overcome with emotion. Rohini had to carry her younger brother during the walk, as he was very young and extremely frightened. The family had to dodge and hide in the forests to avoid being found and detained or killed.

Upon reaching Dhanushkodi, they were registered and taken to Chengalpattu by train, and eventually to Gummidipoondi by bus. Throughout the harrowing journey to India, Rohini was worried as to whether they would reach India safe and secure. She and the rest of the group were in an extremely fragile state of mind.

Rohini recalls that they left everything and ran for their lives to escape the Sri Lankan army, who were killing people indiscriminately. The girls and women from the community were being sexually harassed and raped. The civilians felt caught between the LTTE, the Sri Lankan army, and the Indian Peace Keeping Force (IPKF), and had no one to turn to. In their desperation, they could only think of running to India. They undertook the journey with a lot of trepidation and in mortal fear. To her surprise, they made it to India without any mishaps and were well-received by the local authorities.

Her family and the others were given IDs and ration cards and were told about their entitlements with regard to provisions and monetary allowances. Nowadays, they also have Aadhaar cards, which they received after getting their biometrics done at the local district office.

Rohini says that she is happy in the camp, despite the many difficulties that they face. There is widespread poverty and hardship, even hunger. The people have to live extremely frugally and work in precarious jobs to earn whatever they can and substitute their allowances, which are too low to sustain them. But they are at peace, and they can sleep peacefully without worrying about death and the sorrow it brings.

She becomes emotional as she talks about the helplessness that she feels at times. She says that people sometimes say unkind words, which hurt the self-respect and pride of the refugees. They are constantly worried about their self-image and whether their children would grow up to have decent, respectable lives. Rohini says that sometimes she cries inconsolably as she remembers all that she has lost for no fault of hers. She dislikes feeling like a dependent and being reduced to the identity of a refugee.

But when asked whether she would consider going back to Sri Lanka, she becomes more circumspect. She says that two families from the original group of six families that had travelled from Mannar to India have voluntarily repatriated to Sri Lanka. These two families had support from their relatives and friends settled abroad, who sent them money to relocate and kickstart their lives again.

In the absence of any such support, Rohini thinks that it would be impossible for her and her family to go back to Sri Lanka, even though they often think about it. She has all sorts of fears and apprehensions about moving there and having to start from scratch all over again. Her fears have been further reinforced by people who have returned to India after having moved back to Sri Lanka. These people cite the difficulties that they faced in finding jobs and setting up their homes and the lack of adequate support systems as the reasons for their decision to come back.

Rohini says that she would prefer to continue staying in India and build a good life for her children. She and her husband want to give them decent education in the hope that they will find well-paying jobs and not have to work for daily wages as painters, labourers, etc. She adds that she would rather wait for a better life here than go back to the life of uncertainty and hardship in Sri Lanka. After all, she has had enough uncertainty and hardship to last her a lifetime, she concludes.

Tharani, 41 years

Tharani was born in Trincomallee, in Northeastern Sri Lanka in 1977. Her family included her parents, three sisters and a brother. In 1985, her parents moved to Mannar while she and her siblings stayed in Trincomallee.

Tharani remembers those years to be extremely tense and frightening. She and her family felt stuck in the war between the LTTE, the army, and later on, the IPKF. It was very difficult to trust anyone, and the Tamils and the Muslim community of the North-East were constantly fearful of betrayal. At the time, the LTTE was in control of Mannar, Mullaitivum, and Vavuniya, and the entire area was under attack by the army. Tharani remembers that the day she left for India, the Sri Lankan army bombed Mullaitivu and the person who had helped her escape died.

She remembers that she came to India in 1990 and that it took her nearly six months to get to India from Trincomallee. She left for India with her uncle and aunt and her siblings at the age of 12. Her sister Geetha was 11 years old, and her brother Deepak was 6 years old. The youngest sister Janani was just 2 years old at the time and had lost both her legs up to the knees in a land mine accident. The eldest sister was married and had already left for India much before them.

Tharani and her family made their way by boat to Mudur, 5 km from Trincomallee. From Mudur, they walked along the sea to Mannar. She and the rest of the group of almost 70 people would hide in the forests during the day and walk during the night. They walked for nearly 30 days before they reached Mannar and were able to escape the island in a boat. During the boat journey, the group was afraid that they would be found by the Sri Lanka Navy or sent back by the Indian coast guard. But they were able to land at Dhanushkodi, Tamil Nadu, without much trouble and claimed refugee status by registering themselves at the police station there.

Tharani remembers the help that she received along the way and upon landing in India. She recalls that while the group was walking through the forest, people from the villages along the route would give them food, water, and other utilitarian items. Similarly, people were very helpful in Dhanushkodi.

After registration, the group was taken to Kottaikadu. On the way, the authorities gave them food and INR 100 or 150 for immediate needs. The group was also given vessels for cooking and eating. Tharani and her family initially settled in the camp at Kottaikadu. She went to school in Kadapakkam, which was about 2 km from the Camp. She studied up till 9th grade at the school, after which some of the families living in Kottaikadu were moved to the Thiruvannamalai Camp. Tharani then joined another school near the camp and finished her 11th grade.

Tharani got married in 1995, when she was 17 years old. Her husband Anbu was 28 years at the time of their marriage. They lived at the Nemeli Camp for the first four years of their marriage, and their first son was born there. Tharani fondly recalls that she delivered her son with the help of a nurse who used to visit the camp from a nursing home.

The young family then moved to the Kilputhupattu camp near Pondicherry. This was a relatively bigger camp with nearly 2,000 people.

Tharani and her husband then moved to Nanganallur and rented a house in the city for a monthly rent of INR 450. Their second son was born here.

Tharani got trained in sewing in 2015. She also did a beautician course. She has now set up her own enterprise where she employs four workers on a total salary of INR 100,000. She says that she took a loan of INR 50,000 for starting it and that she has almost 200 regular customers.

She hesitates in answering when asked whether she wants to go back to Sri Lanka. She says that she does yearn to go back but is reluctant because of the uncertainties involved. She feels that she has worked very hard to build a life in India from nothing and has finally settled after many years of moving around and struggling. Now, all of her assets along with her family, relatives, friends, and costumers are here.

Tharani says that she is grateful that her family is safe here and that they can live outside of the camp and be self-sufficient. But she rues the fact that the refugees have to put up with various forms of indignities, especially hurtful words and degrading behaviour from authorities.

She is wary of the stories that she has heard about the people who went back to Sri Lanka and then returned because they could not find avenues to make a decent living there. Unless she is sure of what kind of opportunities exist there for the returnees and of what sort of help they would be provided by the authorities, Tharani is not willing to go back.

Stories from Pakistani displaced minorities in India

Suman Devi, 45 years

Suman Devi was born in Ghotki district in Sindh and came to India in 1998. She has been living in the Kudi Bhagtasni area of Jodhpur with her husband and three children for the past few years.

Back in Sindh, Suman's parents worked as labourers in the fields. She recalls the numerous incidents of assault and robberies that the Hindu families in the area had to put up with. She says that it was common for local Muslim men to snatch money from people from the Hindu community on their way back home after a hard day's work and beat them up if they protested. Sometimes men and children from well-to-do Hindu families would be kidnapped for ransom and killed if the demand was not met. Suman also states that if the Hindu men who worked in factories or farms owned by Muslim landowners ever committed any mistakes, they were tied down and beaten up. All of this contributed to a pervasive sense of foreboding and terror amongst the Hindu families.

But worst of all was the fear that the families felt for their daughters' well-being. Suman and her husband had two daughters who were enrolled in a school nearby and they were always fearful of whether the girls would return home safely. They were constantly worried and under a lot of stress. When they shared their fears with few relatives in India, they were advised to leave Pakistan. Keeping their daughters' safety in mind, Suman and her husband decided that they had no choice but to move to India.

Suman says that they had great difficulty in obtaining visas for the family. It took them almost six months and costed them lakhs, but they finally managed to get them and arrived in Haryana, India. Initially they stayed with their relatives because all their savings had been expended on the visas and travel. But considering their relatives' troubles with money, Suman's husband started working as a labourer and soon moved his family to a small rented accommodation.

Suman narrates the challenges that she and her family have faced since they came to India. Her daughters wanted to resume their studies here but in the absence of identity proofs and adequate documentation, they were unable to get admission into a school. After months of struggle and with the help of their relatives and the local administration, Suman was able to get them enrolled. Suman also started working as a daily wage labourer and together she and her husband were able to meet the household expenses and pay for their children's education.

Suman fondly remembers that one of her daughters was extremely good at studies and wished to pursue engineering. After much effort, they were able to get her admitted to an engineering college. But despite being from a lower caste (Suman's family belongs to the Meghwal scheduled caste), they did not receive any fee concession as they did not have a caste certificate, among other Indian documents.

By this time Suman's family had been living in Haryana for 15 years, yet they had not acquired Indian citizenship. She and her husband were worried for the future of their children amidst all the uncertainty. They had heard that Pakistani Hindu migrants in Jodhpur had mobilised and had been successful in getting citizenship for a few families. So Suman and her husband decided to move to Jodhpur.

Their hardships continued in Jodhpur as it was very difficult to find rented accommodation and decent employment. Her husband finally landed a job as a mechanic in a garage and they were able to rent a house.

In Jodhpur, Suman's daughter, who had been studying at an engineering college, expressed her desire to carry on with her studies. But due to the difficult circumstances of their move, Suman was unable to spare enough for her education. This adversely impacted her daughter, who became withdrawn and depressed. Even after Suman and her family moved into Banar camp, which was set up by the local administration for Pakistani Hindu migrants and started saving on rent, they could not afford to support her studies.

The thought of being unable to study further and fulfil her aspirations started tormenting Suman's daughter mentally. She would not share her pain with her family as she did not want to burden them, but they could sense how distraught she was. One day, her circumstances got the better of her, and Suman's daughter committed suicide.

Suman expresses profound sadness that they were unable to support their daughter's wishes. She laments that perhaps if they had been able to acquire citizenship and had access to rights and entitlements, her family could have had better social standing and financial status and she would not have had to lose her daughter in this tragic manner.

Mala, 40 years

Mala was born in Mirpur Khas in Sindh province. Her parents were agricultural labourers. She had four brothers, two of whom owned a small grocery store in a nearby town and the others worked with their parents in the fields.

Mala says that their daily lives were very oppressive in Pakistan. It was common for Hindu men and women to be assaulted, robbed, and harassed in a number of ways by members of the Muslim community. She talks about a specific incident where her brother was attacked by a few Muslim men on his way back home from the grocery store one night. They took all his money and severely beat him up. They tied him to a tree on the side of the road and left him there in his half-dead condition. Mala's brothers went to look for him when he had not returned till late and found him there.

Mala got married to Prabhu Chauhan and moved to Jamesabad to live with his family. She gave birth to four sons over the years. Mala says that her sons were enrolled in the village school till 5th standard, after which they had to move to a school in the nearby town for higher standards. She narrates that when her son Raghu was in the 7th standard, he started complaining about the discrimination he had to face in school. Most of the students and all the teachers at the school were Muslim and Raghu felt that the Muslim children had more freedoms than the rest. The students were expected to read kalmas and verses from the Quran during the morning prayers. This was compulsory for all students, including the Hindu children. If any child were to resist or complain, the teachers would beat him or her and threaten to get them rusticated from the school.

After listening to her son, Mala talked to the parents of the other Hindu students at the school and they approached the principal with an appeal that the school make provisions for more holistic education and also teach the students about Hinduism. The principal dismissed their concerns and said that if their children wanted to continue studying in his school, they would have to follow its rules and regulations.

Mala and the others then decided to send their children to another school. But the principal refused to issue their children's transfer certificates. As a result, the parents were unable to get their children enrolled in another school.

While the stand-off between the parents and the principal was going on, Raghu got an opportunity to meet the District Education Officer at a book fair. He expressed his grievance before the officer. The officer then called a meeting with the parents and instructed the principals of all schools in the area to accommodate the parents and arrange for the children to be taught about Hinduism and issue their transfer certificates in case any parent wished to admit their child to another school.

The principals acquiesced to his order at the time but did not take any action thereafter. Instead, Mala and Raghu became targets in the eyes of the local Muslim community who were outraged that they had dared to raise this

Narratives of refugee women 51

issue with the authorities. The persecution of the Hindu community escalated, including frequent assaults and robberies and destruction of Hindu shrines.

Raghu even started receiving death threats in the aftermath. Mala and her family were so scared for his safety that they hid him in other people's houses for over a month. Considering his and their other children's future and safety, Mala and her husband decided to leave Pakistan.

Mala's husband approached local agents for their visa documents when their official application was rejected. They spent a huge amount of money but were finally able to obtain the visas and come to India four years ago.

The family travelled to India on religious visas which required them to go to Haridwar through Jodhpur, then Delhi and onwards. The touts who travelled with them had promised to help them in Jodhpur, where Mala's husband had a few relatives. But when they reached India, the touts forcefully extracted more money out of them and sent them to Haridwar under the threat of getting them jailed.

Mala and her family made their way back to Jodhpur with a lot of difficulties. They spent days on the road with little money for their survival. When they reached Jodhpur, they were completely broke and had no place to stay. They remained homeless for days as they could not afford to rent a house and their relatives, who lived in extremely poor conditions, could not accommodate them either. After a couple of weeks, they managed to save enough from daily wage labour to set up a shanty in the camp where their relatives stayed.

But the issue of their children's education for which they had to flee Pakistan could not be resolved here. Their sons could not get admission to any school because they did not have essential documents, including the transfer certificate. Given the difficult financial circumstances of the family, the sons also joined Mala and her husband in working as daily wage labourers.

The children were extremely despondent about having to discontinue their education. The financial situation of the family continued to be very bad as it was difficult for them to get employment. Mala says that they thought of going back to Pakistan many times during this period.

A couple of years later, they were able to receive basic documents with the Rajasthan government's intervention based on the advocacy efforts of a local organisation. This enabled Mala's sons and others like them to enrol in the National Open School and resume their studies.

Mala says that the children continue to struggle to complete their education due to language differences and lack of a support system. Many of them drop out and start doing petty jobs. Mala reflects that it is always very difficult to leave one's home and family and other familiar things to settle in a new place. It has been especially tough for them and other Hindu families from Pakistan as they have no rights or recognition here. She says that life has taken a long time to normalise and is still challenging, but they all put up with everything in the hope that their children will be able to get citizenship in India and pursue their education and livelihoods without any fear.

Jamuna, 42 years

Jamuna arrived in India in 2014 with her children, three daughters, and a son. She is a widow and works as a labourer to run her household. The family lives in a shanty in a colony of Pakistani Hindu migrants in Jodhpur.

Jamuna says that back in Pakistan she lived with her parents who worked as agricultural labourers. She remembers that in her childhood, the financial condition of the family was not good as her parents found it difficult to support their large family on their meagre incomes. But Jamuna's eldest brother was very hard working and attained good education against all odds to become a doctor. He set up his own clinic and dispensary and the condition of the family started improving gradually with the help of his income.

Jamuna narrates that the local strongmen from the Muslim community were envious of her brother's success and they started coming up with various ways to disrupt the clinic's business. They got a tea stall opened in front of the clinic where the ruffians from the village would gather. They would sit at the tea stall the entire day and shoo away patients by threatening to beat them. They would particularly target patients from the Hindu community, even hitting them if they tried to access the clinic. They also put pressure on Jamuna's brother to stop treating Hindus and treat people from the Muslim community for free instead.

The family was getting increasingly distressed and decided to leave Pakistan and come to India. Jamuna's brother applied for visas for the entire family but was the only one who was granted a visa. Concerned for his life and safety, their parents urged Jamuna's brother to leave for India while the others stayed back.

A few years later, Jamuna's husband, who was a construction worker, died in an accident. The sole responsibility of raising their four kids fell on Jamuna and she started working as a daily wage labourer. Shortly afterwards, Jamuna got to know of a heart-wrenching incident that took place in her neighbour's house. The neighbour's two girls aged 15–16 years went missing. The parents ran from pillar to post trying to trace their daughters' whereabouts but were unsuccessful. A few days after the incident, few Muslim men from the village came to Jamuna's neighbour's house and told them their daughters had converted to Islam and would be living with the Muslim community from then onwards. The neighbours suspected that the men had abducted their daughters and sexually assaulted and forcibly converted them. But they were unable to register a complaint or persuade the men to return their daughters.

This incident rattled Jamuna and she started constantly worrying about her daughters. She felt extremely vulnerable, more so as she is a widow, and was fearful that if a similar incident were to happen to her daughters, she would be completely helpless to do anything.

Jamuna then decided that it was time for her and her family to come to India. She talked to her parents and got all the visas and documents arranged with their help.

She arrived in India with her father (her mother had passed away in Pakistan while they were waiting for their visas) and her children. They went to Jodhpur, where one of Jamuna's married sisters was already living with her family in a camp of Pakistani Hindu migrants.

Jamuna had already exhausted her savings and assets trying to get to India and was left with nothing. Seeing her situation, Jamuna's sister asked other camp residents for help and they pooled in resources and built a shanty for Jamuna and her children in the camp.

Jamuna's troubles are far from over, however. In order to make ends meet and raise her family, she again started working as a daily wage labourer like most of the other women in the camp. But the family can barely survive on her meagre earnings. Her children, who were good at studies and were keen to resume them in India, were unable to do so. Moreover, Jamuna has little money to spare in case anyone falls ill or in case any other emergency befalls the family. They continue living in penury and cannot access any public services or entitlements as they have not attained citizenship yet.

Khushboo, 42 years

Khushboo came to India 28 years ago. She has been living with her family in Jodhpur. Back in Pakistan, her father used to sell toys and her mother went from door to door to sell clothes. Her brothers worked at a coal godown. The family lived by modest means but were comfortable.

Khushboo has seen a lot of death and loss around her. She describes an incident from her childhood where men from the Muslim community in their village started pressurising her neighbour to hand over their daughter to them. They threatened to kill the entire family if they did not do so. The family tried to get help from the police but were unsuccessful. Unable to bear the pain and ignominy of the family, the daughter hung herself.

A few days after this incident, Khushboo's cousin (her maternal uncle's daughter) was abducted under similar circumstances. The whole family was helpless when the police refused to file their complaint and there was no way to bring the girl back. Badly shaken by these events, Khushboo's parents decided to leave Pakistan and come to India along with their family. They expended their savings, sold off all their jewellery and other assets, and borrowed money to fund the visa process and enable the journey.

After coming to India, Khushboo and her family stayed with their relatives for a while. Their father was finding it difficult to get a job and they could not afford a place of their own. After 2 years of remaining jobless, her father got a job in a factory. Over the years, he was able to get Khushboo's siblings married. But with the expanding family, their expenses were steadily rising too. One of Khushboo's brothers had incurred a lot of debt in trying to secure his livelihood and support the family. Unable to pay off his debt, he committed suicide leaving behind his wife and two small children.

Khushboo got married shortly after this tragic incident. Her husband was a labourer, and her brother-in-law worked in the vegetable market. Her marital home was not without its woes. Khushboo's sister-in-law had been long suffering from tuberculosis and remained extremely ill. The illness slowly consumed her, and one day she jumped into the river with her little daughter and committed suicide.

Khushboo and her family decided to stay separately from the rest of the family after this as they were worried about the effect the deaths would have on their young children. Her husband continued working hard to support the family, but their financial troubles persisted. As Khushboo's children started getting married, it was becoming more and more difficult to stay in a single room rented house. Unbeknownst to Khushboo and the others, her husband took a loan from the bank to construct separate houses. He started remaining extremely stressed about his inability to repay it. Khushboo says that her husband just left the house one day and did not return. It has been seven to eight years to that day and the family has no idea about his whereabouts or whether he is alive or dead. They believe that the financial stresses of the household got the better of him.

Khushboo now goes door to door and sells clothes to earn a living, just as her mother did all those years ago. But she can barely manage two meals a day and meet the house rent with this income. Although Khushboo has lived in Jodhpur for so many years, she has not been able to acquire Indian citizenship. She does not even have an identity card. Therefore, the means of livelihoods and income available to her remain very limited, adding to the miseries in her life.

Ragini, 50 years

Ragini, her husband Rajesh, and their seven kids arrived in India in 2018. Rajesh used to work as a labourer in Pakistan and they all lived with Rajesh's parents and siblings in a joint family. Rajesh's employer had rented out a *katcha* house to him, where they all stayed.

Ragini says that the family and the larger Hindu community in the area had to put up with various forms of persecution such as robbery, physical assaults, sexual harassment, and forcible conversions over the years. But there was one incident that changed their lives forever.

Ragini narrates that a few men from the Muslim community of the village had taken to parking their big cars in front of the main door to their house. This used to cause Ragini and her family a lot of inconvenience, especially to the women who needed to move in and out of the house multiple times a day for their errands and other work. One day, her brother-in-law, Brijesh, went up to the family members who owned the cars and asked them to remove them and not park in front of their door anymore. Enraged by his insolence, the head of the family collected the male family members and a few others and beat Brijesh up with sticks. They left Brijesh bleeding and half-dead on the road and warned the bystanders to not say anything.

Ragini's sister-in-law and Brijesh's wife, Kamla, found him there in this state and got him admitted to the hospital with Ragini and Rajesh's assistance. While Brijesh was receiving treatment, the men continued to park their cars in front of Ragini's house. A few days later, Kamla was again inconvenienced by one of the cars and she asked the owner to move it. He returned with a crowd of people who pulled Kamla out of the house and started hitting her with sticks. As a result, Kamla fell unconscious. But the crowd's anger was not satiated. They got into the car that had been parked outside of the house and drove over Kamla. They kept driving over her until she was crushed under the wheels and died.

Ragini and her family were in a state of complete shock and anguish. They went to the police to register a case but were turned away without any help. Thereafter, the Muslim men who were involved in the murder came to Ragini's house and threatened them of a similar fate if they approached the police or administration again. Over the next few weeks, their harassment of Ragini's family continued unabated and they started bothering them in various ways.

At this point, Ragini and her family decided that the only way to save their lives was to leave Pakistan and come to India. Rajesh approached a local agent who informed him that it would cost him a lakh for the passports and visas. Ragini sold all her jewellery, and they borrowed money from relatives to somehow collect the requisite amount and pay off the agents. They succeeded in getting the documents and came to Jodhpur.

Ragini says that she, Rajesh, and their kids were the only ones who were able to escape. Brijesh and the rest of their family continue living in distress in Pakistan as they have not been able to put together the money to leave.

At the same time, Ragini also narrates the challenges that they are facing in India. Given their low caste of Bhil and the fact that they are from Pakistan, Ragini and her family have not been able to get a house on rent. They are also unable to get stable employment, which has made it very difficult for them to survive here. Ragini remains extremely worried about the future of her family, given the dire circumstances they face both here and in Pakistan.

Balwanti, 10 years

Balwanti was born in Rahim Yar Khan district, Pakistan, to Savitri and Hemraj. Hemraj used to graze animals and Savitri worked in the fields of a local landlord.

The Hindu families in Balwanti's village were constantly being pressurised by members of the local Muslim community and the Maulvi to convert to Islam. They would attempt to incentivise the local Hindus by promising them property and jobs and threaten them if that did not work. There were also several cases of forced conversions in the village, including Savitri's parents and other relatives who were abducted by village strongmen and had to convert to escape persecution.

In these circumstances, there was a lot of pressure on Savitri and Hemraj and they were living in constant anxiety of being targeted next. Fearful of the threats and harassment, they began thinking about leaving Pakistan and moving to India with Balwanti and her older brother. Balwanti was a small child of only 6 months at the time. Savitri sold off her jewellery and Hemraj borrowed money from his relatives to pay the local agent and obtain visas for the whole family.

While they were waiting for their visas to be processed, tragedy struck. One day, Savitri had taken Balwanti to the fields where she worked, when a few people came and forcefully carried both of them away. The other workers in the field were too afraid to intervene but they hurried back to tell Hemraj of what had transpired. They also informed him that the abductors had threatened to kill Hemraj if he complained against them.

In spite of this Hemraj went to the police station to lodge a complaint, but the police refused to take any action. Then, Hemraj and a few other members of the Hindu community decided to publicise the news in local newspapers and appealed for Savitri and Balwanti to be returned. Seeing the advertisement, a local Muslim politician approached Hemraj and told him that he should give up hopes of bringing his wife back home as she had converted to Islam. He also informed Hemraj that if he were willing to give a written undertaking that he would never attempt to meet Savitri or pursue an investigation, then he could have his daughter back. Hemraj was growing increasingly desperate and was afraid that he would lose both his wife and daughter. In utter hopelessness, he agreed to the conditions set by the politician and Balwanti was returned to him.

Scared that the same fate would befall Balwanti when she grew up, Hemraj escaped to India with both his children in 2009. He arrived in Jodhpur and started living with his relatives.

Hemraj was struggling to make both ends meet. He wanted to rent a house for his family, but no one was willing to accommodate him as he belongs to the Bhil caste. Eventually, he got in touch with a local organisation which works for the rights of Pakistani Hindu migrants and they helped him move to the migrant colony of Kaliberi on the outskirts of Jodhpur. This land was allotted for Pakistani Hindu migrants from the Bhil community by the state government and the district administration due to the mobilisation and advocacy efforts of the local organisation.

Hemraj started working as a labourer and has now succeeded in constructing his own modest house in the Kaliberi camp. Though he is happy that he and his children are not under threat anymore, he is heartbroken at being separated from his wife and at the fact that his young children have had to grow up without the love of their mother. Balwanti still hopes to meet her mother someday.

Stories from West Saharan women in Algeria

Bintou, 32 years

Bintou was born in a refugee camp in Ausserd in 1986. She is a mother of two young children.

She says that although she has not experienced the war, she feels that she has lived through its sad reality through her parents. She has grown up on stories of the war, the casualties and the hardships that it threw up, and the families that were torn apart as a result. She says that her parents were forced to watch their parents die in front of their eyes. They somehow managed to survive the horrors of war with much difficulty.

Bintou thanks God that the war is over but says that there will be no relief in their circumstances unless they live in an independent country where they are able to govern themselves. Until then, their lives are a long-drawn-out period of waiting and coping and hoping for something better.

She shares the difficulties of living in a refugee camp. She says that the residents have to live in extremely harsh weather conditions, be it summer or winter. There is little or no protection from the vagaries of the desert.

She also says that it is very challenging for women to find jobs. Although they are allowed to work as doctors or teachers, their profession depends on their level of education and most women in the camp are poorly educated. Bintou works for youth management in the camp, but she says that livelihood options are very limited, even for men.

Bintou is happy that at least her children are able to receive education up to the secondary level in the schools run inside the camp. She is also glad for the help that they have received from humanitarian organisations. But she shares that the help is not constant as the organisations and their staff keep coming and going; sometimes an organisation might provide support for a year or two and sometimes one might support them only for a couple of months. This adds to their distress as they are almost entirely dependent on humanitarian aid.

She again expresses the sense of futility she feels. She says that she tells the stories of the war and their history to her children in the hope that they would be able to live in independent West-Sahara someday.

Lalla, 58 years

Lalla was born in 1960 and has been living in the refugee camps of Haussa. She was pushed into exile after the outbreak of violence in West Sahara.

She says that she was tortured before she fled and knows of many people who were either detained or killed at the time. She says that she escaped with a big group of people, many of whom died along the way. She recalls that the Moroccan forces chased them through villages and caught up with them. They were then detained and taken to the airport. Lalla and the others were hit until they got on the plane, where they joined many other injured people who were screaming in anguish. The plane took them to Algeria where they were given refuge.

During the journey, she heard many stories from others of how they had been pulled out of their homes and beaten and how their relatives, friends, and neighbours had been clubbed to death.

Lalla says that she was raped at gunpoint by her torturers and that she has met many women in the camps who are victims of sexual violence. The women all share their stories with each other in the hopes of comforting each other, but the pain always remains.

She says that she was not prepared for exile, but it seems to have been her destiny. After arriving at the camp, Lalla finally felt safe. But she had lost her land and her family. She even had to divorce her husband as he had decided to follow another path and not accompany Lalla.

Lalla says that she feels that her days are devoid of hope and her nights are full of shadows of the past.

She was unable to have any children, miscarrying nine times. She says that it's almost as if her uterus did not have any place for hope either. She has also been sick now for a very long time. She fears that she will die without seeing her homeland again. Thus, she continues to be trapped by her memories and is desolate that there is no one to carry on her stories.

Lalla says that when she reads or sees what is happening in Syria on the news, her heart reaches out to the Syrian women who have been displaced from their homes and their lives. She says that she can feel the suffering of those women who are united with her in war and in refuge.

Maoualmin, 56 years

Maoualmin was born in 1962 and has been living in the Smara camp for years. Her daughter Aziza was born in the camp.

Aziza says that she has heard a lot about her mother's childhood and about the war from her mother. Her mother has told her about her grandfathers, who fought in the war and lost their lives. Aziza expresses gratitude that she did not have to experience the tragedies that her mother and many others did but says that she always carries their stories along with her.

She says that Algerian authorities and people have been good hosts to them. They have received a lot of help from humanitarian organisations. Aziza and her friends were able to finish their studies and even attended summer camps and exchange programmes in other countries.

Aziza knows that the war is still not over for people who are living in the occupied territories. She says that she had visited these territories as part of a peace delegation. The people told her they are still facing violence and are not safe even in their own homes. Many of them testified that they were being tortured but would still shout "long live West-Sahara" so as not to give any pleasure to their tormentors.

Even in the refugee camps, the war is omnipresent. Almost all the people living there have lost family members in the war. There are many people in the camps who were wounded in the war and have had body parts amputated. Many of them never recovered from the shock and misery of the whole experience, and remain ill, both physically and mentally. Aziza recounts an incident from her childhood where she and other children were playing near the refugee camp and they came across a bomb that they mistook for a toy. She was about to pick it up when her father ran up to them to check out the commotion and stopped her from doing so, probably saving her life.

Aziza says that despite all the suffering, the youth is optimistic. They are sure that they will be able to return to the homeland of their ancestors. Her hope is fuelled by the fact that the Sahrawis are already living in parts of Western Sahara known as the liberated territories.

But the area is still unsafe. Aziza has heard stories of people being injured or killed by unknowingly stepping on mines which were buried in the desert during the war. These mines are now being surveyed and cleared with the help of other countries. Aziza is grateful for all the attention and support that their cause and their plight have received from the international community.

Maoualmin speaks up and adds that her people have long suffered due to the colonisation. She says that they just want to defend their rights and want to live in their own country with dignity.

She shares that she left her two children back in her homeland when she fled the war. Over the years, she has tried to visit them, but the Moroccan authorities have refused to give her permission. Instead, they offered her money to come back and live with her children, but Maoualmin refused because she does not want to live under occupation. She says that she and the others do not crave the comforts of home or do not simply want to settle down, but they want their land to which their identity is inextricably attached.

When Aziza leaves the room, Maoualmin says that she had been gang-raped by men from the armed forces before she could escape and come to Algeria. She does not want her daughter to know as she would be heart broken. Maoualmin says that rape does not just destroy the victim, but it also destroys the perpetrator. Once you have treated someone like an animal, she says, it is very difficult for both to live as complete humans.

She says that after this incident, she decided to come to the camp alone. Over the years, she has been able to heal. She says that what helped her was the sense of women's solidarity in the camp. She says that so many women have gone through similar experiences that her story could be the story of any one of them; her face could be the face of any one of them.

Maymouna, 40 years

Maymouna Abdellah came to Algeria in 1979 when she was 7 years old. She lived in Dakhla, which is situated in an area that was colonised by both Morocco and Mauritania. When the Mauritanian forces withdrew in 1979, the civilians in the region were also expelled by the Moroccan forces.

Maymouna says that her father enabled them to flee to safety. She left with her mother, sisters, and brothers, one of whom was just a month old at the time. Her father, his mother, and his sister could not escape with them.

Maymouna and her family arrived at the refugee camp where her grandparents and aunts were already staying. She has been in the same camp since. She even jokes that her grandchild now goes to the same school where she went all those years ago. But her face betrays the sadness that she feels at the grim reality of generations having to grow up stateless in a camp. She says that more than anything else, her experience has taught her patience. She has transmitted this value to her children. People who spend their entire lives in tents with the most basic of amenities must learn to be immensely patient and hopeful, Maymouna says.

Maymouna talks about the harsh conditions of life as a refugee. She says that they do not have jobs, so they have to depend on the assistance that they receive from humanitarian organisations. But these organisations come and go; the support is not constant or sustainable, so the refugees find informal ways of surviving.

Most people in the camp suffer from severe health problems. Maymouna has heart problems, thyroid complications, and breast cancer. She says that she is forced to get admitted to the health centre for months at an end. Her mother is also sick. Maymouna's daughter has had to drop out of university to take care of her grandmother. The hospitals are not easily accessible, and the refugees have to travel long distances to get treatment.

Maymouna says that this is what her life has been reduced to. She leaves the camp to travel almost 2,000 km and be admitted to the clinic and then she comes back to the camp when she is discharged. Her younger daughter who was born in 2003 is also sick with rheumatic fever. She is unable to go to school. Instead, she accompanies her mother during Maymouna's prolonged periods of hospital admission.

Since 2006, Maymouna has had to constantly travel because of her ill health. She says that the family has been split up as a result. They are unable to get together even for festive occasions. Her father continues to stay in Dakhla, her mother and daughter are in the camp, while she and her younger daughter are in the clinic for most of the year. When Maymouna underwent surgery for breast cancer, she was hospitalised for more than three months.

She breaks down when she says that in all these years, she has only seen her father for five days, when she went to Dakhla a few years ago. Over the years, they stayed in touch over the phone and he tried to help her family out with money whenever they needed, but now he is too old to work. She says that the meeting was very difficult for everyone. Her father has been suffering just as they have, and he said that he cannot bear this image of his children as refugees. He still remembers his children and his wife as they were when they left Dakhla. Maymouna says that her father could not attend any of their marriages and he was not there for the birth of his grandchildren. The separation weighs very heavily on all of them.

Maymouna says that she and her family have suffered a lot, but they still hold on to the hope of having their own country. Her vision for a better future for her children is intertwined with her desire to see an independent Western Saharan nation. She says that she wishes that their children would not suffer the injustices of colonisation and displacement that they did. She has taught them to have the indelible hope of revolutionaries, as she considers them all to be children of the revolution.

Stories from refugee women in the Democratic Republic of Congo

Malaika

Malaika is from Rwanda and has been living in DRC for over 17 years now. She sells eggs in the streets of Goma to make a living.

She says that she was forced to leave Rwanda in 2001 with her older brother after being gang-raped by three Rwandan soldiers. They found refuge in Walikale, North Kivu, about 200 km west of Goma. Malaika says that she conceived as a result of being raped and gave birth after coming to DRC.

In 2010, armed clashes between the Maï-Maï militia (Congolese rebellion) and Democratic Forces for the Liberation of Rwanda, or the FDLR (Rwandan Hutu rebellion active on Congolese territory for more than twenty years), forced Malaika to move again. She was one among the hundreds of Rwandan refugees living in the eastern part of DRC who were displaced.

Malaika then migrated to Goma and spent two years in a transit camp with her then 8-year-old daughter and 10-year-old niece. She briefly lost contact with her brother while they were fleeing but was reunited with him after the UNHCR located him in Congo Brazzaville.

To meet her family's needs, Malaika has set up a small business. She received help from a programme to support income generating-activities run by the UNHCR through its partner AIDES. She manages to earn about 30,000 Congolese Francs per month to pay her rent for a small two-room house and to educate her two daughters who go to secondary school.

Despite this, she says that she cannot meet all her needs. She laments that her children were unable to get their school reports for the year, as she could not pay the entire school fees. This incident made Malaika very anxious and fearful about their future, as she considers education to be the path to a stable life and to self-reliance.

Malaika is also scared that her daughters might have to face sexual violence as they grow up. Trying to suppress her pain, she prays that her children never have to go through what she has endured.

She reflects on her experience of living in DRC for so many years. She says that the Congolese are nice people but some of them regard the Rwandan refugees with suspicion and think that they might be members of militia groups such as FDLR.

In Goma, refugees live side by side with the local population and have integrated into the economic circuit. But there is a deep fear and distrust of

Rwandans among the inhabitants which has been instilled due to the presence of the FDLR rebels who have been accused of carrying out various crimes and atrocities against civilians in North and South Kivu. Malaika is afraid of what might happen to the Rwandan refugees if such prejudices and confusion persist.

Despite the success of the UNHCR's voluntary repatriation program for Rwandan refugees, many of them say that they are not yet ready to leave. Malaika is one of them. She says that she did not flee the war but the other dangers that continue to thrive in Rwanda. She becomes pensive and sad at the reawakened memories, not daring to reveal the evil that haunts her.

Ruth, 71 years

Ruth has been living in Goma since 2010 and operates a small business for sealing coal from her two-room house. She is originally from Uganda, from where she was forced to flee under the tyrannical regime of Idi Amin.

Ruth and her family left Uganda in 1971 with tens of thousands of other people, both Ugandan and foreigners. She says that her family was forced to leave everything and run when Idi Amin started targeting ministers, officials, judges, diplomats, university professors and teachers, businessmen, journalists, etc., whom he considered to be sympathetic to the former regime or a threat, including her husband. They ran to Tanzania and lived there for 37 years as refugees. They received support from the UNHCR and were slowly able to rebuild their lives and even bought a house.

In 2008, Ruth and her family returned to Uganda as her husband wanted to revive his political career. The return trip was quite smooth and comfortable, unlike the terrible journey for exile in Tanzania. The family sold their possessions, including the house, and invested the money into her husband's election campaign.

But things started going horribly wrong and her husband was killed a few months later. Ruth was at the hotel where they had been staying when she received the news that her husband and two of her children had been murdered along with 50 other people. Ruth fell unconscious and had to be taken to the hospital where she was revived.

While she was in the hospital, she discovered that her two other children had also gone missing during the attack that killed their father and brothers. She later traced one of them to Mozambique and the other one in Tanzania with the help of UNHCR. Ruth stayed at the hospital for a few days and survived with the support of other patients, doctors, and the Pastor who regularly visited the hospital. They would make sure that she ate, shared her sorrows, and prayed with her.

The Pastor suggested that she should leave for the DRC. His brother-in-law was staying there and would be able to welcome Ruth.

In 2009, Ruth arrived in Bukavu in the DRC, before making her way to Goma. She says that when she arrived in Goma all alone, she did not know anyone except the stranger whose phone number had been given to her by the Pastor, referring to his brother-in-law. At the port, she was met by the young man who took her to the police and then to the UNHCR. Ruth then received her refugee status and joined the ranks of the thousands of refugees hosted by the DRC.

Ruth was provided with assistance from the UNHCR to launch a revenue-generating activity, with which she started her small coal business. But she says that the assistance and her income do not allow her to meet her basic needs.

Ruth has diabetes, stomach pain, and high blood pressure among other age-related ailments. She needs to get proper care and maintain a decent diet. But it is impossible for her to pay for her treatment, manage her diet, and pay the rent.

Ruth is really struggling to make ends meet. She says that many times she has to go to bed on an empty stomach.

Yet she smiles to hide her pain and the burden of the harshness she has faced in life. She is unable to maintain her jovial veneer when she thinks of her two surviving children, however. She fears that she would not be able to catch up with them and will die without seeing them again. Her eyes fill up with tears as she holds a picture of one of her sons in her hand and stares into the void.

Ruth is unwilling to return to her home county, despite memories of the beautiful life that she was forced to abandon. She says that she has nowhere to go and no one to return to and that her home does not exist anymore. Her parents were killed during the regime of Idi Amin, and their house has been taken over as state property.

Instead, Ruth dreams of going elsewhere. She says that she would like UNHCR to find her another country of refuge where she can get better care. She says that there is no peace in DRC either and she is afraid of what will happen due to recent political unrest.

Meanwhile, she continues to eke out a living from her business and devote the rest of her time to prayer.

Amina Tabeya

Amina fled from Burundi in 2015 when violence broke out in the country in the wake of the national elections. The crisis led to widespread killings and gross human rights violations. She and her family arrived in Bukavu, DRC, and are now living in Goma.

No one is prepared to flee, she says grimly. People can never imagine giving up their possessions, their livelihoods, and their homes and leaving until they are forced to do so.

She recalls the confusion, fear, and hatred that had gripped people in the first few days of the war. Amina's brother-in-law escaped from his house and came to them in search of safety. He was soon followed by members of one of the warring factions, who pulled him out of the house and shot him. They then asked Amina's husband to help them load his body onto a truck. One of the men ordered her husband to follow them and he never came back. Amina says that she has since had no news of him and is not sure whether he is alive.

Amina and her sister, whose husband had been killed, then escaped with Amina's children. In the chaos that ensued during the journey, Amina lost one of her children. She and the others tried to find the child for days but to no avail.

Amina is now trying to rebuild her life in DRC with the help of UNHCR and the local authorities. But every day brings with it huge struggles. She is completely dependent on the aid and income support that she receives. She says that she sometimes feels like the UNHCR is the father of her children; if she continues receiving support from them, her children would be able to live peacefully and happily, and if she is abandoned by them, her children would be utterly vulnerable and impoverished.

She is also grateful to the Congolese government for its support. Amina says that if a refugee is arbitrarily arrested or assaulted, the National Commission for Refugees (CNR) gets involved and attempts to find a solution.

But she also feels that the moment people get to know that someone is a refugee, they become cautious and wary of them. Locals seem to be afraid of refugees suspecting them to be spies or militia members. Amina talks about how the chief of the neighbourhood where she lives constantly supervises her. He even eavesdrops on her conversations when she has visitors and is unwelcoming towards her and her family.

In these circumstances, it is difficult for her to imagine what kind of a future her children will have. She is worried about their education and their livelihood prospects. For now, she is determined to do the best with what she has and ensure that her children are safe and happy.

Jacqueline Habonimana, 42 years

Jacqueline Habonimana fled the Burundian inter-ethnic war of 1972 as a little girl and came to Rwanda.

She recalls that her family had to flee almost overnight on foot. They crossed the border tired, afraid, and empty-handed.

Jacqueline grew up in Kigali in Rwanda. She got married there and gave birth to two daughters. When the violence broke out in Rwanda in 1994, she and her family were again displaced forcefully.

She says that as the news of the death of President Habyarimana (the then president of Rwanda) spread, the Burundian refugees living in Rwanda decided to escape to DRC. Jacqueline's younger daughter was only 6 months old when they left with others from the community.

Jacqueline has had to fight very hard against the circumstances to survive. She says that when they fled, she once again lost everything she owned as they left all their belongings and loved ones behind. During the journey, many of her friends and acquaintances died as a cholera epidemic broke out. During the journey and even after it was over, she witnessed immense suffering and trauma.

She fled with the documents that UNHCR had given them when they were living in Kigali as refugees. With UNHCR's help, she was able to register herself in the DRC with the National Commission for Refugees. Over the years, she has received some financial help from the UNHCR. She has channelled part of that money into setting up and consolidating her hair-braiding business.

She also started sending her children to school and the UNHCR helped her in paying their school fees. She proudly states that her second daughter has finished her graduate studies and that Jacqueline paid the university fees from her own savings from the business.

But she is extremely worried about the future. She explains that life is very difficult in the DRC. She and several other refugees are struggling due to the lack of livelihoods and widespread poverty. It is only by the grace of God that my children have access to nutrition and education on account of my braiding work, she says. She adds that her children are scared of going out and of mingling with the local children. Even when they go out for a walk, they stick to the short distance between her and her neighbour's house.

Jacqueline is grateful for all the assistance that she has received from UNHCR and from local authorities. But she reiterates the challenging circumstances that she faces. She says that it is not every day that they get help, and ultimately, they have to work very hard to ensure that the little financial support that they receive translates into financial independence for them and their families.

Safi Misago

Safi Misago arrived in Uvira in South Kivu, DRC, from Burundi in 1993. She fled as the inter-ethnic violence between Hutus and Tutsis became so violent and widespread that the neighbourhoods of her city started to empty out as people were fleeing en masse.

She painfully recalls the many losses she has suffered. Her parents and brothers were killed during the war. She says that she ran out of her house to escape, without knowing which direction to take. She crossed the border with no possessions, not even an ID, and found herself in Uvira.

After living in Uvira for four years, Safi shifted to Goma in North Kivu, DRC.

She talks about the challenges of being a single mother in these difficult circumstances. She says that many Burundian women fled with their young children, often two or three in number. Due to the lack of livelihoods and any institutional support in Goma, they have become extremely vulnerable to sexual exploitation and domestic abuse. There are several instances where women have become pregnant and have been abandoned by their partners, and they have no access to a home or a stable source of income to be able to support the child.

Safi has benefitted from a small livelihood programme run by the UNHCR. She says that the money she received enabled her to open a small business and pay for essential needs such as food and school fees. But as her children are growing up, her worries are increasing. She laments that the money she makes is not enough to cover their expenses, especially as their studies are becoming more expensive. She has very little savings and has been unable to invest back into the business and consolidate her earnings.

She also talks about the sense of alienation she feels. Although refugees live with local communities in the city, there is a palpable lack of trust and tension among communities. The proliferation of armed groups in the region, including militias of Burundian origin, has made matters worse. Safi says that refugees are constantly afraid of being targeted or being denied services.

Although she has personally never had problems with her neighbours, Safi is saddened by the lack of comfort and familiarity. She says that people who were not well off in Burundi could still eke out a living with the support of family and other community members. For example, one could borrow retail items from the local shopkeeper and sell them, and then split the profits. People were also able to find housing at cheaper rents through their contacts and networks. But for refugees, these social networks are almost non-existent.

She feels that life is extremely hard for refugees living in the DRC. The entire region is in a constant state of instability and flux marked by widespread poverty, conflict, and political unrest, and refugee communities are adversely impacted by the lack of safety and economic opportunities. She feels helpless as she cannot go back to Burundi, where things continue to be volatile after a recent outbreak of violence in 2015, and she feels unsafe in DRC where the sociopolitical realities are very similar. She now hopes to be resettled with her family in a different country.

Stories of internally displaced women in Syria

Mirvat Saleem Naqqar, 45 years

Mirvat was captured by armed militiamen who invaded Adra, a suburb of Damascus, Syria in December 2013. She spent four and a half years in captivity.

She says that on the morning of the invasion, she and her husband were awoken by the sound of gun shots and people shouting. They started panicking and trying to figure out what was going on, when they were told that their town had been surrounded by armed forces and that they should stay indoors.

She saw the armed men standing outside her window. They were in multitudes and spread out everywhere. They started breaking into homes in large groups and shouting sectarian slogans and firing on people. Mirvat could hear the sound of doors being smashed as well as the shouting and crying of the inhabitants. She could also see civilians, mostly men and boys, being pulled out into the street and being shot or decapitated. She saw children being thrown off the rooftops of buildings. The armed men also set shops and houses on fire, burning alive entire families. The magnitude of destruction and slaughter around them was unimaginable, Mirvat says.

Mirvat and her family were trapped inside their homes. They were extremely scared, and they could see that the armed men were shooting people who tried leaving their homes. After two days of occupation, the Syrian army started bombarding the area.

On the third day, the armed men entered the building in which Mirvat and her family lived. They were specifically searching for people from the Alawi sect. They broke into Mirvat's house and took her husband Jaafar away. Mirvat tried to follow him but was stopped by her neighbour's son. Jaafar never came back. Instead, the armed men came back and robbed their house and took away their car.

Mirvat and her children spent the night in their neighbour's house. The next day the armed men came back and asked for Mirvat by name. She held her children close to her and told them to not tell the armed men that she was their mother, as she had seen what the armed men had done to the children of the people they were targeting. And then she walked out. She was surrounded by the armed men, who detained her and took her to the police station in Adra along with few other women. The police station was full of men, women, and children who had been imprisoned there.

Mirvat says that the prisoners were degraded and humiliated by the armed men. They would beat the prisoners with electric cables. They would torture the young men in front of the room where the women were kept, so that the women could watch. They would force the boys to get half naked and then spray them with icy water in the cold weather. They would lash them with whips, kick them, and maul their heads with their boots.

A few days later, the police station was bombed by the army and the prisoners were taken to another location. This became a pattern – the army would bomb the building where the civilians were being held captive, so the armed men would quickly move them to another area where the torture would continue. Mirvat says that it was as if the armed men could convert any place into a torture chamber within minutes.

When the Syrian army surrounded Adra, the captives were put in a basement. They were held there for six months. Mirvat says that during their captivity, it felt like time had stopped and that they were tasting death every day.

The prisoners were perpetually hungry and thirsty. Their food consisted of four spoons of burghul (a type of grain) and polluted water full of leeches. The armed men would hit the women with electrical sticks if they heard any children crying. They forced the men into hard labour, digging tunnels. Many of the prisoners died during this period because of the torture and harsh conditions.

Mirvat was especially targeted by the armed men as she and her husband had worked at the Atomic Energy Institute. Her captors suspected that she had valuable information. Moreover, many of her relatives such as her brother, uncle, and brother-in-law are serving in the Syrian army. So she was interrogated by them regarding information about her work and about her relatives. During the interrogation, they would whip her and even broke her toes. They would also threaten to capture her children and kill them in front of her eyes.

As the Syrian army got close to where they were hiding, the armed men escaped with the prisoners through a tunnel. They were taken to Duma, where they were distributed into three groups and handed over to three different armed rebel groups.

Mirvat was in a group that was taken by Jaish al-Islam. She and the other women in the group were put into the basements of the Agricultural Research Institute, which had been transformed into a prison.

She says that the torture intensified in Duma. There was a huge lice outbreak, and all the prisoners were forced to shave their heads. Yet they were not allowed to clean themselves or shower. They were left for seven months without showering. Their skins became thick with dirt and grime.

The torturers would remove the nails of their victims or cut small parts off their bodies. They would leave their victims dying in agony or wait for them to recover so that the torture could begin all over again. They would torture the young men in front of the women and force the prisoners to watch videos of torture. Such psychological warfare was very important to the torturers and gave them much pleasure. Mirvat narrates an incident which damaged her deeply. She says that there was an old lady among the prisoners. The captors killed her two sons, who had been soldiers in the Syrian Army. They cut off their heads and brought them to the old women and put them in her lap. She went mad with shock and grief.

Mirvat continued to suffer at the hands of her captors. They whipped her with electric cables, burnt her with coal, removed her toenails with pliers, and broke her hand. She was put in solitary confinement for three years. The armed men would sometimes put her in a cage and place her on the rooftop when the area was being bombarded by the army. Yet she somehow survived all of it. She started concentrating on keeping her sanity. She would observe everything going around her, including the fighters. She would steal books that the armed men would collect for burning for heat and would read them to distract and mentally stimulate herself. She also focused on helping other prisoners out whenever she could.

Finally, they were able to escape when the Syrian army bombarded the building. Most of the militiamen escaped, leaving the prisoners to fend for themselves. Some of the prisoners died during the bombardment but the others were rescued and brought back to Damascus, where they were reunited with their families.

Mirvat says that the scars from her injuries are still visible. She feels broken inside but has regained strength since she reunited with her children. She feels that she must be strong for them as she is the sole parent now.

She says that her children suffered a lot while she was away. Her son, who has a hearing problem, is dependent on her in many ways. When she came back, she found that his health and psychological condition had deteriorated. She says that the pain of captivity pales in comparison to how she feels when she sees him like this.

Mirvat has now got her job back at the Atomic Energy Institute. She says she is concentrating on working hard and earning a decent life for herself and her children. She spends most of her energy on helping them study and do well at school.

She believes that Syria has become a war theatre for international powers and the agency of the Syrian people has completely been destroyed. But she adds that the war was unable to break their spirits. She hopes to support her children and help them build a safe, secular, and secure country.

Ghadeer Haytham Al-Sett, 30 years

Ghadeer left her house seven years ago with her husband and their children. They used to live in Babilla, in the periphery of Damascus. When the war began, they fled to Nahja, also in the periphery of the city.

She recounts the terror of the days immediately after the fighting began. Her neighbourhood was being bombed and her friends and family were trapped. One day, they saw a missile fall in front of the gate of their building. A little girl died in her father's arms in the explosion and the father lost his legs. After this incident, Ghadeer and her husband were desperate to escape for the sake of their fearful children.

They walked through their neighbourhood along with her husband's family until they reached Al-Qazzaz. From there, they were able to find a ride which took them to Nahja. Due to the circumstances in which they left, they could not take any of their belongings with them.

Ghadeer's husband used to work as a scaffold carpenter in the construction sector. She recalls that he would earn a decent living and they led a comfortable life.

Her husband and his brothers joined the Syrian army as volunteers when the war broke out. Her husband did not survive.

Ghadeer's brother too was serving in the army. He was abducted by ISIS (the Islamic State) and she has had no information on his whereabouts since. Her maternal cousin was also taken away by armed militia. She says that she is aware of many similar cases of disappearances and abductions, especially of men, who either joined the fighting or were killed.

As a single mother in a conflict zone, Ghadeer has faced several hardships. She registered herself with the government programme to receive aid, yet in all these years she says that her family received aid only two or three times. She continues to struggle to make ends meet. Despite the challenges, she is relieved that she and her children are alive. She says that all she wishes for as the war seems to be ending is for God to give her the strength to carry on in order to raise her children.

Samira Mahmoud Arnaout, 50 years

Samira lived in the Taqqadam neighbourhood of Damascus. In December 2012, she left the house with her husband to go to the hospital for his kidney dialysis, when armed clashes broke out between the Syrian army and ISIS in her neighbourhood, and they were unable to return.

She and her husband went to her daughter's house in Bab Mosalla neighbourhood of Damascus and stayed there for three months. Thereafter, they moved to Bassima, on the periphery of Damascus. When the situation deteriorated there as well, she and her family moved to another suburb called Daff al Chok, where she continues to stay till date.

Samira's husband used to work as a bus driver with a tour company, while she worked at home. She would occasionally take food orders from women in the locality to supplement their income. Two of her sons used to work as metalsmiths, and the youngest one worked in a falafel shop. She also has two daughters, both of whom are married. She says that they owned their house and used to live a comfortable life.

But the war has completely upended Samira's world. She lost her husband as she was unable to take him for kidney dialysis sessions on a regular basis. His health deteriorated because of inadequate care, and he passed away a few years ago. Her sons are now serving in the Syrian army and Samira does not see them for long periods of time.

Her youngest son Mahmoud was abducted by ISIS fighters in 2016 and has not been heard of ever since. Her daughter's husband was also killed by ISIS in Palmyra, where he had been volunteering with the Syrian army.

Samira says that she has had to support herself and her children's families since they were displaced. When she and her husband moved to Daff al Chok, they started staying in a small abandoned shop. Samira again started taking food orders from the other families who were settled in that area and set up a small business. Her husband, who suffered from diabetes and had previously lost one of his legs to the disease, was unable to work and was completely dependent on Samira. She could not bear the high expense of his medical treatment. They were helped by a charity for a few years as they paid for the husband's treatment.

Samira sees her elder son Ahmad whenever he is on leave from the army. Her middle son Mohammad was caught in the fighting in the city of Deir Ezzor for two and a half years but is now back in Damascus and comes to meet her on his days off.

Samira has been tirelessly trying to find Mahmoud since he was kidnapped. She approached his military base but found out that they had declared him to be a deserter due to some confusion regarding his transfer papers. They refused to help her look for him. She then went in front of a military judge to convince him of the misunderstanding and request him to intervene. She even went to the office of the International Committee of the Red Cross to ask for help. She is still waiting to hear back from someone and is desperate to get any news of him.

Samira's widowed daughter and her children were also displaced after the conditions in their locality worsened. Samira becomes extremely sad as she talks about all the death and destruction that she has seen around her. She says that she has witnessed the destruction of their homes, their beloved neighbourhoods, and their city. She has seen people get brutally injured or die due to the mortars of the rebels and the bombings by the army. There was no relief or haven for civilians anywhere.

Samira says that while the area was under ISIS control, she used to be scared and anxious all the time. She would not cooperate with them and tried to avoid coming in contact with them as much as possible.

Once the army started moving in, the security services took over the abandoned shop where Samira and her family had been staying, and they were displaced once again. But she managed to find an apartment on the same street and moved her family there. The house has a high rental fee and is in poor condition. But Samira is grateful that she has a roof over her head and a place to run her business from.

She struggles a lot to make ends meet but is adamant to provide for her eight grandchildren. She shows her chafed and cracked hands as proof of the grinding hard labour she has to undertake. But in spite of everything she has been through, she hopes for her grandchildren to receive a proper education and live decent and honourable lives with their families. She also hopes to be able to go back to her home someday and for her country to become safe again.

4
A FACE TO THE JOURNEYS

From the pages of an artist's sketchbook

Molly Crabapple

In late September 2015, Doctors Without Borders/Médecins Sans Frontières (MSF) invited me to document their work in Domiz camp in Iraqi Kurdistan. Run by the UNHCR, Domiz was home to over 40,000 mostly Kurdish Syrian refugees. Over five days, I drew MSF's maternity clinic, where they helped 660 mothers give birth in the first half of the year, as well as their mental health groups and community outreach. As I worked, the Syrian refugee crisis dominated the news. Countless refugees would start their journeys in Domiz. In collaboration with MSF, I drew portraits of some of these families, which were published as an article in *VICE* magazine.

The refugees live mostly in tents or cinderblock shacks (though I saw one made solely of tin). The schools are overcrowded and limited. What few jobs exist pay little. Due to funding shortfalls, food rations given by NGOs had been slashed. Yet those who lived there did their best. Some grew gardens. One man I met ran a business faux finishing the shacks to look like stone. In the dust, a wide variety of shops blossomed: wedding dress rentals, satellite dish repair shops, cafes offering massive portions of hummus. The woman running a tiny convenience shop refused to let me pay for a bottle of water. It was a hot day, she said. When power fails, as it does six hours a day, the heat can drive one to madness.

I visited eight families that were planning to make the trip to Europe. Though each of their stories was different, each of these visits began the same. A young person would brew us coffee, served in frail, lovely cups. One of the parents would say they had made the decision to leave. They knew the risks. They read the news of course; some had neighbours who had drowned in the Aegean. They would tell stories of selling all their possessions to afford the smugglers' fees, of following cousins across Europe via messages on WhatsApp, of asylum applications, of daughters who wanted to be doctors and sons who missed their soccer teams in Qamishlo.

DOI: 10.4324/9781003047094-4

When these families decided to take the trip to Europe, they were choosing many things, but one was an individual destiny. They would not wait passively in a tent for geopolitics to decide their fate. They would take matters into their own hands. Theirs was a longing to live.

I asked one woman what she would bring with her to Europe. She looked at me, smiling slightly at my thickness.

"As a souvenir," I clarified. "To remember."

She answered, "I left all my memories in Syria."

A community health worker and his mother living in the Dohuk Refugee Camp. People are keen to leave the war and destruction behind and travel to Europe to rebuild their lives and guarantee their children's future.

A face to the journeys 75

A Syrian family preparing to leave for Europe. Refugees are willing to spend all their savings and borrow on top of that to flee despite the uncertainties that they are likely to face, including the threat of detention and deportation.

76 Molly Crabapple

A Syrian woman and her daughter prepare to leave for Europe. "My journey is dangerous, and I am afraid of it".

A face to the journeys 77

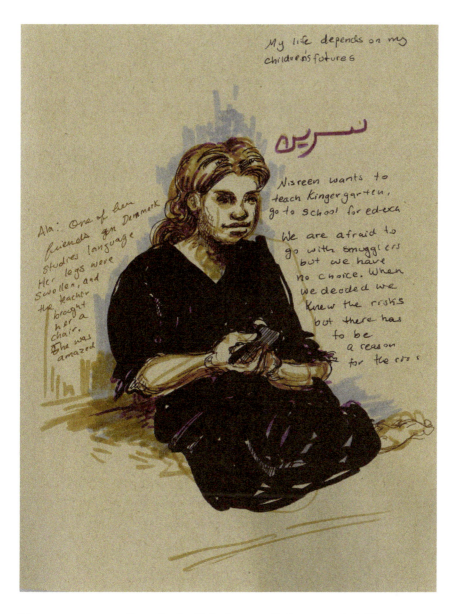

Nasreen, a young refugee in the Dohuk camp. Refugees pay their life savings and take on debt to hire smugglers who they know are often liars and thieves. During their journeys, refugees risk kidnapping, extortion and rape.

A young Syrian health worker. In the absence of legal and safe routes, people risk kidnapping and death on the road without knowing whether they will be able to get asylum on the other side.

A Syrian family waiting in the Camp. Many refugees remain stuck in overcrowded and unhygienic camps, where it is difficult to access food, water, work, electricity, and ensure the protection and well-being of their loved ones.

80 Molly Crabapple

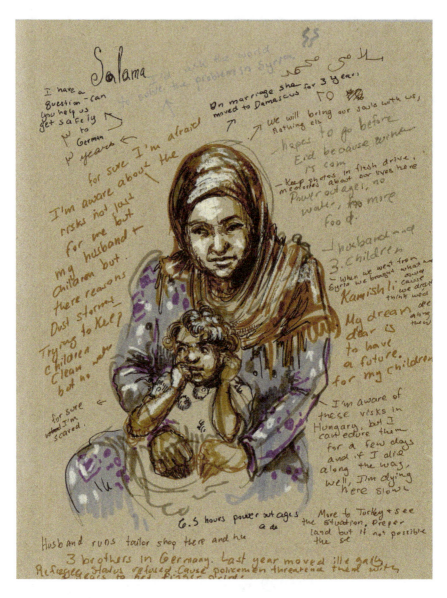

Salama and her daughter. In the face of debilitating conditions in camps, refugees are willing to endure the unimaginable. "If I die along the way, well, I am dying here slowly".

A face to the journeys 81

A family discusses leaving for Europe. Health issues, including trauma-induced stress and mental illness are common in the camps due to deprivation and poverty, state of surrounding conditions, and a pervasive sense of hopelessness about the future.

The Suleyman family. Family separation is also common, as people may get separated while fleeing or might be forced to split up in order to look for work or asylum in another country.

A face to the journeys **83**

A health worker speaks with an expectant mother in a maternity clinic run by Doctors Without Borders. There are several expecting and new mothers, and single women who have been widowed, separated, or abandoned in camps who need special care and assistance, but may not always get it.

84 Molly Crabapple

A little girl is born in the Doctors Without Borders Maternity Clinic.

A midwife soothes a new baby at the Doctors Without Borders Maternity Clinic.

Little Ayat in the waiting room at the Doctors Without Borders Maternity Clinic. "Can you take her to Germany?"

A face to the journeys 87

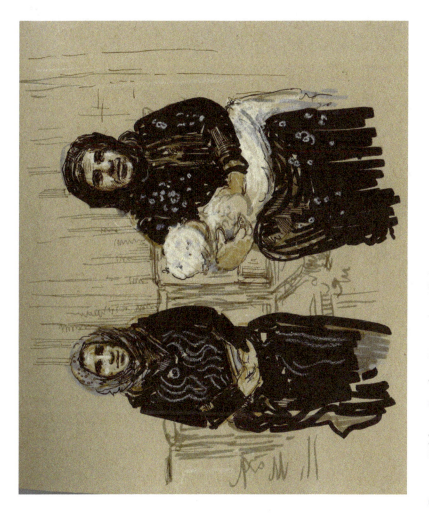

Mothers wait at the Doctors Without Borders Maternity Clinic.

A cleaning woman at the Doctors Without Borders Maternity Clinic. Despite the harshness and despair around them, refugees continue to struggle to write their own destiny.

A face to the journeys **89**

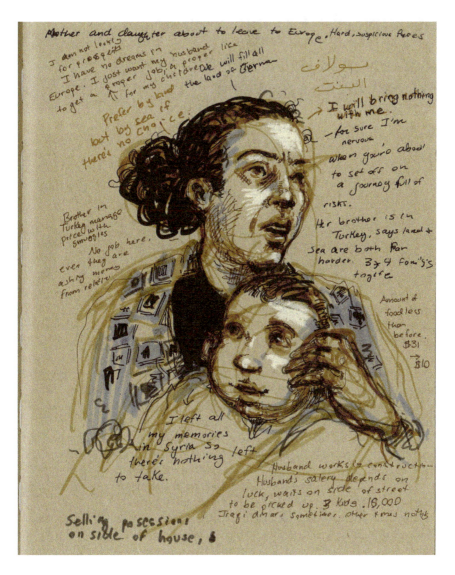

A mother and her daughter prepare to leave. "I left all my memories in Syria. There's nothing left to take." Asylum seekers are not looking for prosperity but to be able to survive.

5
ROHINGYA EXODUS 2017

A photo essay on life at refugee camps in Cox's Bazar, Bangladesh

Mahmud Rahman

The Rohingya exodus started on August 25, 2017, and I travelled to Ukhiya in Cox's Bazar, Bangladesh, on September 20 to understand the plight of the disenfranchised and displaced minority.

Between September 21 and November 2, 2017, I spent seven weeks in the camps (mostly Balukhali camp and Moinar Ghona camp) collecting stories.

I had my first encounter with Rohingya families landing at Shah Porir Island on September 25, a month after they first began arriving in Bangladesh. This was the entry point while travelling over the *doijaa* (sea) from Myanmar. I heard from some of the families that they walked for days and reached the edge of the water only to encounter boatmen who were charging them "an atrocious amount" to carry them to safety. But with no possibility of turning back, they had little choice but to pay the steep fees.

Their harrowing tales reminded me of my family's past. My father escaped persecution in Assam, India, in 1967, and we ended up in Dhaka, Bangladesh, all those years ago. Our family – my parents and five children between the ages of 2 and 9 – survived crossing the mighty Brahmaputra, the deceptions and challenges on the road, and starvation in search of safety.

Watching young Rohingya mothers dragging themselves with their children in tow, I had flashbacks to my own journey. We were lucky that we all survived and found a home in Dhaka. But, what the Rohingya have suffered is incomparable to my family's experience.

I have seen people arriving tired, with vacant eyes, looking for help. I have seen their eyes light up with the faintest glimmer of hope.

DOI: 10.4324/9781003047094-5

The faces speak of the journeys made. The girl's eyes in the photograph above show the fear of her unfamiliar surroundings. These are not experiences meant for children.

"I delivered my son outside a villager's home, two hours after crossing by boat into Bangladesh. I was not that afraid. The shame – that was something else. The whole delivery was outside, and they just covered the place with tarps as some people were looking. I was screaming a lot. They didn't have proper bandaging, so I bled through my clothes for two days. It was very shameful," said Senowara.

The land we were born in is not our homeland. The village our mothers raised us in is burnt to ashes. We crossed a river and are now stranded on a hillock. Where do we go from here?

Mojibor, 16, and his younger sister, Rubina, 7, are both crippled by polio. Their father was shot in front of the children, says their mother. The children were carried by the elder cousins and uncles during the long walks through the hills. "We left no one behind; we suffered but carried on to reach the border line on the edge of the water."

Somira arrived at the camp two weeks ago with her extended family. Her son is almost 2 years old and her new-born daughter is 1 month old. Somira is 19 years old. "I do not like it here," she says.

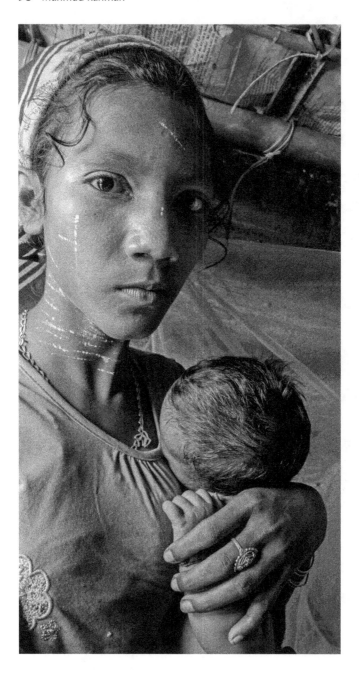

"The firing started on our way to Bangladesh and everyone was running. I could only grab my siblings. My mother was carrying our 15 days old brother. We have been in the camp for three weeks and no one can tell us whether our parents are alive or not. The little ones ask for mother and I tell them that she will come soon." Rubina has a food card and cooks for her siblings, already a caregiver at 15.

A young Sisyphus. Would you send your little one, not much taller than the bucket he pulls, to fetch water?

A Rohingya mother, being carried on a stretcher made of a donated saree to the big hospital. The mobile clinic could not help her.

Noor Kaida, Noor Fatema's 2-year-old daughter, died this morning of fever and swollen throat. Noor Kaida is 20 years old and is married to Rashid, who is also unwell. "While we were on the run, it rained often, and my child caught a cold. Reaching the camp, the doctors gave her medicine three times, and no one charged money." It was dusk when the child was taken for burial and Noor Fatema was taken to the hand pump below for a "cleansing bath."

"Women order dresses and that brings money for our family of ten members. We both finished 4th grade and then were forbidden to continue, as it was the common norm among Muslim families in Myanmar." Mofiza and Mokaroma work as seamstresses, both girls want to continue their work but are reluctant to go out to work.

Children learning *Memar Bing Akra* (the Burmese alphabet) in a school in the camp. "I am the English teacher while there is a Burmese teacher also. I have passed my metric exam in Myanmar and I have been chosen to work as a teacher," says Arfan.

"While there is life, there is hope." Marcus Tillius Cicero

6
FEMINISTS ON THE MOVE

Priyali Sur

Abeer[1]

Syria – Turkey – Greece – North Macedonia – Serbia – the Hungarian border, 2015

> With each passing day there are fewer safe places in Syria. Everyday decisions whether to visit a neighbor, to go out to buy bread have become, potentially, decisions about life and death.
>
> —Paulo Sérgio Pinheiro, Chairman of the United Nations panel investigating human rights abuses in Syria[2]

It was the summer of 2015. The war had been raging for four and a half years now. More than 200,000 people had been killed. In the capital city of Damascus more than 3,700 civilians had died in the fighting between government forces and insurgents. Tanks and military trucks in the city had now become a common sight. Some small parts of the city still bore a semblance of normalcy with shops, schools, and banks open but mostly it looked like a fortress. Abeer was used to seeing soldiers in the streets and checkpoints within Damascus by now. She worked as a manager at a bank and many of her colleagues had either fled the country or were planning to do so. But she didn't know a life outside Damascus. She was born here and had lived here for 48 years, had met and married the love of her life in this city and was now a grandmother to two beautiful boys. Her eldest son was in his final year of medical school and his wife worked as an accountant at an Italian private clothing company. Her other son was studying computer engineering and her youngest girl, 16-year-old Aya, was in high school. She was proud of how she and her husband had worked hard to give their children a good education. She loved Damascus; she loved the city with its old architecture, the

DOI: 10.4324/9781003047094-6

mosques, and the parks. She enjoyed her shopping trips with her close friends to the old city, where they would stop for coffee and catch up on gossip at the Nawforaa cafe. Abeer hoped the war would end soon and she and her family could go on with their lives.

So, one evening when she and Aya were stopped by soldiers at a checkpoint, the reality of the war hit her even harder. A young male soldier walked up to her daughter Aya and said "A beautiful girl like you should not be out. Why don't you come with me?" Abeer had heard stories of women being harassed and molested at checkpoints, especially women whose identity cards mentioned the city of Daraa. Daraa was the stronghold of the anti-government rebels where the uprising had sparked, ultimately leading to the civil war. Thankfully they were from Damascus but was that good enough to protect them? Both her heart and mind were racing now. What if the man took Aya away from her? Her child, her beautiful daughter. She couldn't let that happen. Aya didn't say a word, fiddling with the edges of the hijab around her chin; she kept her eyes lowered at her feet. Abeer knew she was helpless. Moments passed and thankfully both mother and daughter were allowed to go with no further harassment, but that experience shook Abeer. She went back home that night and told her husband for the first time that they should consider leaving Damascus – leaving their home.

Leaving Syria was not just difficult but also very expensive. The Assad government was arresting and detaining those who showed any form of dissent. Many men had been abducted and had gone missing. Women started forming groups to leave together. Many planned to get to Europe and then apply for family reunification for their men. Abeer and her husband started to consider all these options. They managed to speak to a smuggler. The cost per person would be between USD 4,000 to USD 5,000. That meant USD 40,000 for a family of eight. They could not afford that. That would strip them off their retirement savings. They decided to lie low, avoid routes and neighbourhoods where the war was in full swing, and hoped that this ordeal would end soon.

For another month things seemed to be moving along. It was not peaceful, but they were surviving and building for a future when the war would be over. Then one afternoon Abeer's oldest son was arrested and taken away. His friends said that Assad's soldiers came and grabbed him and a few other boys from the medical school. By the time Abeer and her husband reached the police station, it was too late. They were told that he had been shot dead. Some said that there had been a mistake. They got the wrong guy they said, but no amount of reasoning could bring back her son now. She blamed herself. She had stayed for too long. What if they had left a month ago? Her son would still be alive.

Sitting at the steps of the police station, waiting to know when they could get her son's body, she realised that this was not her Damascus anymore. It was a war zone where her son had been murdered. She quit her job, the family gathered all their savings, and once again those who could help them make the move were contacted. They were given strict instructions to not carry more than one small backpack per person. The men were advised to stay back. The women would move together in a group, making it easier for them to get to Europe and then apply for family reunification for the men. But all of this came at a risk. There had been too many stories of people being shot, drowning to death, or dying of exhaustion. Abeer, her daughter, and her daughter-in-law with the two little boys were leaving everything behind. Leaving their homes, their lives, but the hardest was to leave the men in the family behind – her husband and her younger son. She promised them that she would get there soon and apply for their papers. They didn't know how long it would take and when would they see each other again. But this wasn't the time to think, this was the time to leave.

Almost a month after Abeer left Syria; she lay on a tar road, at the border crossing between Serbia and Hungary. Shivering in the cold night, she was wrapped up in what looked like an aluminum foil blanket handed over by humanitarian workers. She had made her way all the way from Syria to Turkey, Turkey to Greece, and then walked all the way to North Macedonia, through Serbia and was now at the Hungary border. The guards at the refugee camp in Macedonia had been brutal. The woman standing in front of Abeer in the queue to the toilet couldn't understand the language the guards spoke. So, when they asked her to stay in the line, she stepped out instead and took her little boy to the toilet as he needed to go urgently. This was seen as an act of defiance by the guard, who then beat her up with a baton in front of her son. Abeer was shaken up by the mindless brutality. Now she, her daughter Aya, and daughter-in-law Noor lay next to each other, trying to keep each other and the kids warm. They were too tired to think what would happen next. Hungary had closed its borders, forcing the refugees to go back. They were trying to think of alternate routes to go further to either Germany or Netherlands.

Shabana[3]

Afghanistan – Turkey – Greece, 2015

A thousand miles away from the Horgos-Roszke border in Hungary where Abeer and her family had hit a dead end, 22-year-old Shabana was about to get aboard a rubber boat from Asso in Turkey. She had left Afghanistan two months ago with her husband, two-year-old son Amir, and parents-in-law. The journey had been excruciatingly painful. Seven-months pregnant with her second child and with an abusive husband, Shabana hoped that Europe would offer her children a better life away from the war back home. She also hoped that her husband would be less abusive in a new country.

She remembered the extremely difficult days of her journey to Turkey. Walking in the snow and in freezing temperature for long, she thought her two-year-old boy would die. He had turned so cold and stiff. One night after an entire day of walking, she and her husband had an argument. It ended the way it always ended – Shabana being beaten up. That night he tried to pull out her fingernails. The exhaustion and the abuse were too much to endure. Somewhere around midnight in the middle of nowhere and with no medical help for miles, Shabana went into labour, two months before the due date. After hours of labour, a tiny frail baby girl was born. Exhausted, Shabana held her to her chest and promised to herself and her baby that they will both survive. She will survive and get to a country where she can give her daughter a better life than hers, a life she deserves.

Now two months later, holding little Ada in her arms and her son Amir, she knew she had come so far but she still had to cross the sea to get to Greece. Just as she was lost in her thoughts, she spotted the smuggler trying to fix a hole in the rubber boat. There had been too many cases of people drowning on those boats. She shouted out to the man and told him to change the boat or she would not get in. He dismissed her and said it was her choice and that this was the only boat available. She and her family had already paid him USD 1,400 per person just to cross from Turkey to Greece. Reluctantly she got into the boat, holding her kids close. A boat meant for about 30 people was carrying more than 50. Just a few weeks earlier the world was shocked and shaken by the image of little Alan Kurdi found dead on the beach after drowning. Shabana had seen that image. She now feared that her children would meet the same fate.

The weather was good and the water welcoming but everyone on the boat was scared. Closer to Greece, water started flooding into the rubber boat. The woman next to Shabana started reciting the Quran loudly; soon others joined her. Many were crying – men, women, and children. By now the water had reached Shabana's chest. She handed over her daughter to her husband and asked him not to let go of their children come what may. Shabana did not know how to swim but she knew she was not ready to die at just 22. She would fight the waves for as long as she could and try to get to the shore. The shore wasn't too far now but the water in the boat kept rising. Much to everyone's relief a rescue boat spotted them, and they were all moved to safety. Shabana and her family were finally in Europe – the island of Lesvos in Greece.

Shabana had to stay in Greece. As an Afghan refugee her chances of resettlement in a European country were much lower than that of other refugees. Shabana and her family stayed at the Moria camp in Lesvos for more than a year. Camp life was awful. It was over flooding with refugees. There weren't enough cabins for everyone and so she and her family slept out in a tent in the cold. There were no doctors and the food could make anyone fall sick. To make it worse, there was violence within the camp. Syrians and Afghan refugees would get into gang fights all the time.

One afternoon, as Shabana was sleeping in her tent, a man walked in and tried to molest her. When she shrieked for help, he ran away. She later found out that the man was a member of another faction and wanted to even the score with her husband, who by now was a member of the Afghan gang. She worried for her family and her children every day.

After a year, they got the approval to move to Athens. She was much relieved to leave the camp. The capital city of Athens was more welcoming. People smiled at her and there were murals around the city that said, "Refugees are welcome".

She felt slightly at ease. For the first time in her life she got a job offer – as a caregiver with an NGO that worked with refugees.

Back home in Afghanistan her husband would have never approved of her working but here things were different. Besides, he didn't have a job, so she had to work to provide for the family. The new-found agency and independence felt so good to Shabana. She wondered if this would change things between her husband and her. Would he now respect her? Would he stop beating her? Would her son Amir be raised respecting his mother and other women? Only time would tell but she knew that just this reassured feeling was worth everything that she had endured.

Biba[4]

Niger – Libya, 2010

> *The unforgiving conditions of the Sahara Desert mean that a broken-down vehicle is often a death sentence for migrants. Most die of thirst after being abandoned by their smuggler.*
>
> —BBC[5]

Biba had been on the road for three days now. Her water ran out on the second day itself. To survive the journey and reach the other end alive, she knew she needed water. Every additional drop of water that she took from others cost her money. Some people were better prepared. They were carrying 20-litre jerry cans tied to the smuggler's vehicle that they were travelling in. A cap full of water from the jerry can was sold for 25,000 CFA (USD 50). A drop of water was literally equivalent to a breath of life in the Sahara.

Biba had never wanted to leave her little village Say, south east of the capital city of Niamey. If she could, she would live, work, and raise her children there. Her parents were farmers, but the 2005 drought followed by another acute one that year (2010) had left them with nothing. It was a hand-to-mouth existence and sometimes even worse. Her parents could never afford an education for her; the opportunity cost was too high. She did odd jobs as a little girl to earn a few francs for her parents but now she was a grown 27-year-old woman and had two children of her own from her first marriage. She did not want them to grow up just rolling in the red mud and dust of her village. She wanted them to go to school and then to Niamey and have good jobs. To make all of this possible, she knew she would have to follow her new husband to Libya. That's where the jobs were. The country had an autocratic leader but ranked the highest in human development index in the African continent. Biba knew that many people had died during the journey across the desert. They had either died of thirst or were killed by bandits. But she had to take a chance. If she stayed back, she and her sons would die of hunger. She had always considered herself to be strong and resourceful, never shirking from doing physically challenging work. So, she knew she could do this, but her little boys, six-year-old Izrafil and three-year-old

Muhammed would not be able to endure the journey. So, she left them with her mother and set out to cross the Sahara Desert by herself, with a bottle of water and some money for the journey. She paid the smuggler at Agadez 100,000 CFA (170 USD) to get her a seat in the next truck to Libya.

They started at the crack of dawn. The Toyota pickup truck was not very big but was packed with more than 20 people. Biba squeezed in. For three days they didn't stop and moved through the desert endlessly. Everyone prayed that the car wouldn't break down. The stress and starvation made Biba sick and to make matters worse, she started her period. Her body ached as she sat squeezed there between others for hours and hours. On the fourth day the pickup came to a sudden halt. It was just past noon and the sun above was scorching. The driver ordered everyone to get off the truck as there was a hill upfront. He asked them to run behind the vehicle up the hill. Those who wouldn't manage to get up there would be left behind. Biba stretched her aching legs. She was thirsty and sick. The hot sand and gravel burned her feet, but she knew she had to run up. She saw others starting to run behind the vehicle. Hastily she tried to move her legs and her body towards the others but in a few minutes collapsed to the ground. In her delirious state she thought – thank goodness my sons are not here. I might die today but at least my boys will live. A few minutes passed and then two other Nigerien women stopped to give her water; others lifted her and carried her to the vehicle. In the truck, women sat tightly around her, so she wouldn't fall out. Sometime the next day they reached the Libyan border town of Murnanna. She was still alive.

On leaving home

> *no one leaves home,*
> *unless home chases you to the shore*
> —Warsan Shire, a British poet and teacher, born to Somali parents in Kenya

Be it Abeer, Shabana, Biba, or any other refugee woman, leaving home is never the first choice. Letting go of the comfort of being with one's own people, of being surrounded by one's own culture, and moving to find safety in another country is often a very conflicted decision. It is when these women are pushed to the edge because of a personal tragedy or threat to life that they finally decide to move. Each of them is well aware of the costs of leaving – the loss of identity, the loss of their homes, savings, and property, and worst of all separation from their family and loved ones. If leaving is hard, the journey is harder.

Refugee women on the move face bias at many levels. The intersection of their various identities – of being a woman, a refugee, a person of color, and their religious faith makes them most vulnerable. They are often targeted by smugglers and traffickers, subjected to abuse along the way, at camps and shelters. With most camps overcrowded, lacking adequate toilets and showers, and with poor access to doctors and medical care, living at camps for prolonged periods (sometimes over a year) while waiting for their refugee status to be determined is nothing short of imprisonment. Be it at refugee camps or in new host communities, integration remains challenging at many levels.

Most refugee women juggle multiple responsibilities – taking care of their children, learning a new language spoken in the host country, doing odd jobs to earn money, and attending school to access better livelihood opportunities. Despite their hard work and the steps taken by them to integrate and feel accepted, most refugee women face rejection from host community members. At schools and workplaces, they are seen as the "outsider" and ridiculed for their clothing, food, and language. The anti-refugee and anti-immigrant rhetoric pushed through conservative and populist political parties adds to the negative narrative around refugees. This makes integration for refugees in local communities all the more challenging. For refugee women, fleeing conflict and desperate conditions at home is not the end to their problems, it is in fact just the beginning of a long set of challenges up ahead.

In Libya, Biba was feeling anything but respected. It wasn't easy being a woman, being black and being a migrant in a new country. Even things like shopping that are meant to be a feel-good experience made her cringe. When Biba would walk into shops in Libya, the women there would cover their noses with their hands. When she left the shop, the shopkeeper would spray it with perfume. They didn't want to touch her, be near her, or even get her whiff. Was this what she had left her children behind for? Was this worth almost dying in the Sahara for? Two years had passed since then and Muammar Gaddafi had been killed. There was violence everywhere. Armed rebels roamed the streets with weapons, randomly choosing houses to raid. One night they stormed into Biba's house and put a gun to her husband's head. They gave away everything they had earned in the last three years and begged for their lives. That night the rebels left but Biba knew they could come back again. And this time they would have nothing to give them.

With nothing to give, the only price to pay would be with their lives. Biba and her husband decided to return back home to Niger. They knew what awaited them back home – poverty and hunger; but at least it was their own home. At least the people there would not detest them, not treat them as slaves, and not be out to kill them. On her way back in a similar pickup truck, crossing the Sahara once again – Biba thought to herself, perhaps it is better to die of hunger than to be killed as a slave. Who knows?

Notes

1 September 15, 2015: Roszke-Horgos Hungary and Serboa border. Interview conducted around midnight at the border crossing.
2 Karen Yourish, K.K. Rebecca Lai and Derek Watkins. Death in Syria, *New York Times* Report. September 14, 2015.
3 September 2017, Athens, Greece. Interview conducted over three to four days.
4 May 2019, Niamey, Niger. Interview conducted over three to four days.
5 Martin Patience, BBC News. The Harsh Sahara: Over 40 people die of thirst in Sahara Desert. June 1, 2017.

PART III
The particular vulnerabilities of refugee women

7
PROTECTION GAPS FOR WOMEN AND GIRLS IN REFUGEE CRISES

Jane Freedman

Despite a range of international conventions, policies, and programmes being in place that aim to prioritise gender issues and the protection of women and girls in refugee crises,[1] and despite the commitment by UNHCR and other international organisations and NGOs to gender mainstreaming[2] in their operations, the grim reality is that for many of these women and girls, huge gaps in protection remain at all stages of displacement and forced migration. Women and girls should not be perceived as essentially or naturally more vulnerable than men, but structural and systematic gender inequalities, before, during, and after forced migration, act to put them into situations of risk and insecurity. These insecurities faced by women and girls relate not just to physical and sexual violence, but also to social, psychological, and economic forms of inequality and vulnerability.

Lack of protection begins with the failure to foresee or prevent sexual and gender-based violence (SGBV) in conflict and emergency situations. Frequently, gender-based forms of violence and persecution are a cause for women's forced migration. In conflict situations, women often experience sexual and gender-based forms of violence, including rape, which forces them to flee to seek international protection. Whilst the international community has started to pay more attention to SGBV against women during conflict, for example, through the various UN Security Council resolutions on women, peace, and security, there is still absence of adequate protection for women against this type of violence. Many of the refugee women interviewed for this book had experienced sexual violence during the conflicts in their countries. Malaika,[3] for example, a refugee from Rwanda, was forced to leave her country and flee to the Democratic Republic of Congo in 2001, after being gang-raped by three Rwandan soldiers. She became pregnant as a result of the rapes and gave birth to her daughter after arriving in the DRC.

Sexual violence against women can also be used as a way to force civilian populations to flee. Roshida Begum, a Rohingya woman, now a refugee in

DOI: 10.4324/9781003047094-7

Bangladesh, recounted the violence used by the Maghs in Myanmar against the Rohingya women and girls. "They were raped, their hands were chopped off and their breasts were cut off. Sometimes their throats were slit, and they would be left for dead." Other women had lost husbands or family members to violence, forcing them to flee to protect themselves and their remaining family. Ruth, for example, was at a hotel in Uganda where her family had been living after returning from a previous period of exile in Tanzania, when she received the news that her husband and two of her children had been murdered. Roshida Begum lost her eighteen-year-old son. The military killed him and threw his body into the river, and although she looked for it for three days, she could not find it.

Forced migration and displacement may also make women more vulnerable to SGBV, including in situations when they are waiting to flee or trying to arrange their journeys. The fact that women generally have fewer economic resources than men, can expose them to risks of violence from the smugglers who they must frequently turn to, to help them flee. Ayesha Begum from Myanmar explains for example that a boatman refused to help her cross the river to Bangladesh as she did not have any money to pay him with. She was forced to wait on the riverbank until her parents found her there about two weeks later with money for the crossing. There are many examples of smugglers asking for sexual favours in exchange for their help when women do not have the economic resources to pay them.

Dangerous and physically challenging journeys can also take a particular toll on women, especially those who are pregnant or travelling with young children. Rohini from Sri Lanka describes her journey to India:

> She remembers that they had to walk for many miles along the seashore to reach the boat. She recalls that as soon as they got into the boat, some of the people fainted due to tension and exhaustion. Her sister, who had a newborn baby of only forty days old, was overcome with emotion. Rohini had to carry her younger brother during the walk, as he was very young and extremely frightened. The family had to dodge and hide in the forests to avoid being found and detained or killed.

Forced migration also leads to the separation of families, and women can be separated from their children and find it hard to be reunited. Whilst it would be wrong to essentialise women's role as mothers, it is clear that separation from children, and sometimes not knowing what has happened to these children, can be psychologically very difficult, along with the added trauma of forced migration. Ruth, from Uganda, had to bear the murder of her husband and two of her children; and lost her two surviving children during displacement. Whilst living in the DRC, she managed with the help of UNHCR to trace these two surviving children to Mozambique and Tanzania, but she still has not been physically reunited with them, and fears that she will die without seeing them again. Maoualmin from Western Sahara shares a similar story. She left her two children in her homeland when she fled the war and came to Algeria. Over the years, she has tried to visit them but has been prevented from doing so by the Moroccan authorities. This kind of trauma, and the inability to be reunited with separated children, is common and a major source of anxiety for many women refugees, and one that is not sufficiently addressed through systems of international protection.

Many women find themselves seeking protection even within the refugee camps. Refugee camps may be envisaged as zones of protection for the populations within them, places where they will be safe from the conflicts they have fled, but these camps may also be zones of violence and conflict.[4] Various studies reveal the degree to which sexual and gender-based violence is a widespread and global phenomenon in these camps.[5] Specific problems arise for women within the refugee camps both because of material factors, such as the lack of essential resources, and because of the gendered political and power structures that exist within the camps. Although efforts have been made to ensure "safe" spaces for women within many camps, there are still camps where a lack of separate washing facilities, for example, makes women feel insecure and exposes them to risk of violence.

The spatial organisation of the camp structures the women's management of their time and shapes the social routines and income-earning strategies of refugees, in particular women. Access to health care, food, and other services may be concentrated within one area in the camp, which facilitates the work of the staff of the UNHCR and NGOs but can be inconvenient and potentially dangerous for refugees and can exacerbate women's workload.[6]

Sometimes this organisation may put women at risk of violence, for example when they have to go outside of the camp to look for firewood. Gathering firewood is generally designated as a task meant for women as it is they who are responsible for cooking and they usually have no choice in the type of fuel they can use to light fires to cook with. The dangers associated with going outside to collect firewood have been documented in relation to a number of different refugee camps in various countries. In addition to the dangers of violence incurred whilst collecting firewood or water, women are also faced with a lack of resources for their basic needs. Again, as it is women who are principally responsible in these situations for feeding their families, it is they who often bear the brunt of the problems involved in managing with the very scarce resources they receive.[7]

The violence and insecurities of life in refugee camps has also been shown to lead to increasing familial restriction and control on girls' and young women's mobility. For example, among some Syrian and Rohingya refugees, displaced families in refugee camps have chosen early or forced marriage for their daughters as a strategy to cope with economic hardship or perceived risks of sexual violence.[8] The women interviewed, who had daughters, expressed fears about their futures, and the risks of sexual violence they face. Malaika explained that she was scared that her daughters might have to face sexual violence as they grow up. "Trying to suppress her pain, she prays that her children never have to go through what she has endured." This view is reinforced by research by the Women's Refugee Commission that highlights the particular insecurities for adolescent girls within refugee camps. These girls "are concerned about a range of issues affecting their lives, including various forms of physical insecurity, barriers to education, limited peer and social support, poverty, overwork, and inability to meet their basic needs."[9]

Frequently, women who are forced to flee find themselves alone, or in sole charge of their children. This places a further economic burden on them, as they struggle to find the resources not only for their own survival but for that of their children as well. Roshida explains that one of the major challenges she faces is to ensure a decent life for her children. "Being a single mother to small children, she does not have a source of income or support." Similarly, Jamuna, a widow from Pakistan with four children, and now living in a shantytown refugee settlement in Jodhpur, India, finds economic survival a struggle. She works as a daily wage labourer.

> But the family can barely survive on her meagre earnings. Her children, who were good at studies and were keen to resume them in India, were unable to do so. Moreover, Jamuna has little money to spare in case anyone falls ill or in case any other emergency befalls the family. They continue living in penury and cannot access public services or entitlements as they have not attained citizenship yet.

Not all refugees find places in camps or even wish to live there. Although life in camps can be restrictive and difficult, life outside is also complicated, with fewer guarantees of distribution of food or shelter. Refugees who are living outside of camp settings, and who do not manage to obtain residence permits, or citizenship in their host countries, are extremely vulnerable, and find it even harder to gain employment, and to earn a living. For example, Khushboo, a refugee from Pakistan who has been living in India for 28 years, lives in Jodhpur with her family. Her husband took a loan from the bank in order to try and construct a house for the family, but one day he left the house and did not return. Khushboo believes that the financial stress of the household got the better of him and led to his disappearance. Khushboo now goes door to door and sells clothes to earn a living.

> But she can barely manage two meals a day and meet the house rent with this income. Although Khushboo has lived in Jodhpur for so many years now, she has not been able to acquire Indian citizenship. She does not even have an identity card. Therefore, the means of livelihood and income available to her remain very limited, adding to the miseries of her life.

There is a major lack of medical and psychological support services for women refugees, and particularly for support for those who have been victims of sexual violence. The traumatic effects of this type of violence last for a long time, but many women might find it difficult to talk about it. And for far too many, there is no suitable psychological support or counselling to help them to recover. Lalla from Western Sahara was raped at gunpoint by Moroccan forces as she fled from her home. Whilst she has reached safety in a refugee camp in Algeria, the pain of the sexual assault still remains. She recounts that she has met many women in the camps in Algeria who have suffered from similar sexual violence. "The women all share their stories with each other in the hopes of comforting each other, but the pain always remains." The lack of psychological support is one of the reasons that women can have great difficulty in overcoming their trauma and may feel continually haunted by the violence that they have experienced. Malaika explains that she becomes "pensive and sad at the reawakened memories, not daring to reveal the evil that haunts her", whilst Lalla says that "she feels that her days are devoid of hope and her nights are full of shadows of the past."

Gender roles and relations may be transformed during forced migration, and whilst this may lead to increased autonomy and new opportunities for some women, for others this is not the case. There is evidence that forced migration may exacerbate incidences of domestic and interpersonal violence. But too often, women who are victims of these types of violence are unable to access help or support to leave their abusive partner. They may be scared to report domestic violence because of fear of reprisals or exclusion from their community group. They may also find that they have no means of economic survival if they leave an abusive partner. Few refugee camps have adequate structures or procedures in place for dealing with cases of domestic violence or for supporting women to survive after leaving abusive partners.

Ayesha Begum's story is illustrative of the ways in which changing gender relations, and changing relations between spouses, can have a negative impact on women during forced migration. She fled to Bangladesh from Myanmar with her children whilst she was four months pregnant after the Maghs attacked her village.

> Ayesha now stays in the camp with her children and her parents. She says that she is suffering a great deal as her husband does not take care of their family. He has remarried and lives in the camp with his second family. Ayesha complains that her husband tortures her emotionally and mentally. She narrates that her husband took her elder son away from her without informing her. She looked for her son everywhere in desperation and found out that he was with his father. She begged and pleaded with him to let her take her son back, but he refused.

Women refugees are also often faced with severe economic problems and have difficulties in providing for their needs and those of their children. Ruth has chronic illnesses and is struggling to make ends meet and to support herself.

> Ruth has diabetes, stomach pain, high blood pressure among other age-related ailments. She needs to get proper care and maintain a decent diet. But it is impossible for her to pay for her treatment, manage her diet and pay the rent. Ruth is really struggling to make ends meet. She says that many a times she has to go to bed on an empty stomach.

Worries about their children's future may be particularly acute for women, who fear that they cannot provide sufficiently for them. Education is a very common source of worry. Malaika, who has set up her own small business, explains that whilst she earns enough to send her daughters to school, she cannot meet all their needs.

> She laments that her children were unable to get their school reports for the year, as she could not pay the entire school fees. This incident made Malaika very anxious and fearful about their future, as she considers education to be the path to a stable life and self-reliance.

Even when refugees have been living in a host country for many years, fear and distrust amongst the host population may still remain. Women expressed the difficulty and insecurity of living faced with hostility and discrimination from local populations. Malaika talks about her life in Goma in the DRC where she has lived for over 17 years.

> In Goma, refugees live side by side with the local population and have integrated into the economic circuit. But there is a deep fear and distrust of Rwandans among the inhabitants which has been instilled due to the presence of the rebels belonging to the Democratic Forces for the Liberation of Rwanda (FDLR) who have been accused of carrying out various crimes and atrocities against civilians in North and South Kivu. Malaika is afraid of what might happen to the Rwandan refugees if such prejudice and confusion persist.

Whilst they may dream of returning to their homes, women also realise that often this is not a realistic possibility as their security would not be guaranteed in case of such a return. Roshida Begum underlines the important point that humanitarian and international agencies such as the UN must ensure their protection if they are to return to Myanmar. She warns that just because she and her family managed to escape to Bangladesh after the most recent spate of violence, it does not mean they would survive further violence if they are sent back.

Unable to feel at home or secure in their new host countries, and equally unable to return home because of ongoing violence and conflict in their countries of origin, many women hope for resettlement to a more stable and welcoming country where they could build a secure future for themselves and their families. Ruth still dreams of finding another country of refuge after spending 17 years in the DRC. But resettlement options for Ruth, and for many women like her, are rare. The countries that do welcome refugees for resettlement have limited quotas of those that they will accept. And there is often a reluctance to accept refugees like Ruth who have serious medical needs.

Having outlined all the protection gaps for women and girls during refugee crises, we should also highlight that whilst these gaps push women into situations of vulnerability, these women in turn also show immense strength and resilience. Mirvat, a 45-year-old woman from Damascus in Syria, was imprisoned and tortured by armed groups for four and a half years. Her husband was taken away and never returned. But Mirvat has returned to Damascus, has been reunited with her children, and has resumed her job at the Atomic Energy Institute. She is determined to work hard to provide a decent life for herself and her children and says that the war was unable to break their spirits. Other women, while still displaced, find strength in solidarity. Maoualmin explains that over the years that she has been in camps in Algeria, she has been able to heal.

> She says that what helped her was the sense of women's solidarity in the camp. She says that so many women have gone through similar experiences that her story could be the story of any one of them; her face could be the face of any one of them.

Notes

1 UNHCR's first *Guidelines on the Protection of Refugee Women* were released in 1991, and since that date there have been a range of other policies and guidelines from UNHCR and other international organisations concerning the protection of women and girls during forced migration and displacement, and during humanitarian emergencies.
2 Jane Freedman (2010), "Gender Mainstreaming in Refugee Protection."
3 The examples referred to in the chapter are from the narratives presented in Chapter 3 of this book.
4 Wenona Giles and Jennifer Hyndman (2004), *Sites of Violence: Gender and Conflict Zones*, Berkeley: University of California Press.
5 Women's Refugee Commission (2013); Ulrike Krause (2013).
6 Jennifer Hyndman (2000), *Managing Displacement: Refugees and the Politics of Humanitarianism*, University of Minnesota Press; Awa Mohamed Abdi (2016), "Refugees, Gender-Based Violence and Resistance: A Case Study of Somali Refugee Women in Kenya," *Women, Migration and Citizenship*, London: Routledge, 245–266.
7 Linda Kreitzer, "Liberian Refugee Women: A Qualitative Study of Their Participation in Planning Camp Programmes," *International Social Work* 45, no. 1 (January 1, 2002): 45–58.
8 Charles and Denman, 2013.
9 Women's Refugee Commission (2013).

8
SOCIAL AND CULTURAL ISOLATION OF WOMEN IN REFUGE

Shahanoor Akter Chowdhury and Sharmin Akther Shilpi

Our Nights are Full of Shadows of the Past and Days Empty[1]

Introduction

Women of all ages experience loss of home and property, loss or disappearance of close relatives and loved ones, family separation and disintegration, and sexual abuse at the time of displacement.[2] A major outcome of the abuse and deprivations they face is that women who are forcibly displaced are among the most vulnerable groups in relation to experiencing loneliness.[3]

After arriving in the host country, refugees face a completely alien and uprooted life in a new environment. This situation, as well as discriminatory or unfriendly government policies in the host country, can add to the refugees' trauma and damage their well-being. Restrictions on entitlements to welfare services and prohibition in employment and mobility, along with the possibility of detention or removal are some of the factors that are connected with stress and loneliness and further impact a displaced person's health and well-being. Refugees may feel discriminated, excluded, unloved, and lonely.

Women and girls are particularly disadvantaged. They are at risk of different forms of exploitation in displacement such as early or child marriage, forced marriage, survival sex, trafficking for commercial sexual exploitation, and forced labour. The fear of abduction, harassment and sexual violence severely hampers their freedom of movement, which results in lack of access to service information, social support networks, and safe alternatives for those under threat of harm at home.[4]

Deep-rooted patriarchal values and conservatism may further restrict women and girls from decision-making. This negatively impacts their lives and puts them in an adverse situation where men or the collective community make choices and decisions for them and for their families.

DOI: 10.4324/9781003047094-8

Due to these existing inequalities, gender discrimination, and unequal power relations, displacement hits women the hardest and the recovery period is also longer for them. In times of humanitarian crises, maternal mortality rate, sexual and gender-based violence (SGBV), and sexual exploitation of women increase drastically. Women lose access to health services such as family planning, pre-natal care, and postpartum care. Women often lack opportunities in accessing education, life-skills trainings, and livelihoods and this lack of opportunities is usually exacerbated in a displacement context. In addition, their needs and demands are generally ignored or unrecognized and there are fewer resources dedicated for women to rebuild their lives. The above reasons contribute to lengthening the recovery period for them, especially when it comes to women-headed households and single women.

This chapter discusses the multi-faceted social and cultural isolation of women who are in refuge.

Conflict, violence, and trauma

Conflict-induced displacements make women and girls vulnerable to distinct forms of violence. One key reason for this is the general breakdown in the law and order situation during conflict, which leads to an increase in all forms of violence. In addition, the culture of impunity towards violence against women in many societies becomes more entrenched in conflict situations and encourages men to be more aggressive and show misogynist behaviour. Unaccompanied women or children, young girls in foster care arrangements, and single female heads of households are all frequent targets. Elderly women and those with physical or mental disabilities are not spared either.

Maoualmin, a West-Sahara refugee, living in Haussa camp in Wilaya Smara tells the horrific story of war:

> You know the war is horrible. It is in the past, but it is still there. You can meet many people who lost all their family members during the bombardments. Many people are sick because of the war. In the refugee camps, you can meet many people who are war-wounded, war amputees.[5]

Maoualmin was brutally gang-raped. She says,

> You asked me if you can take a picture of me and I refused. It's not because I am afraid to be known as the one who has this horrible story. It's because my face is not important, my destiny is important. My face can be the face of any woman.

War and displacement have thus physically and emotionally damaged refugee communities; many people in the camps have lost limbs, are frequently unwell, and carry physical and psychological scars. The World Health Organisation (WHO) estimated that in situations of armed conflicts throughout the world,

"Ten per cent of the people who experience traumatic events will have serious mental health problems and another ten per cent will develop behaviour that will hinder their ability to function effectively." The effects of refugees' traumatic experiences are immeasurable, long-lasting, and shattering to both their inner and outer selves.[6]

Women carry the weight of the trauma of the violence they have been subjected to before and during the time of displacement and in the camps, often by themselves. This results in a feeling of isolation among the women and might cause mental health issues, of which the most common are depression, anxiety, and psychosomatic problems such as insomnia, or back and stomach aches.[7]

For example, Rohingya women in refugee camps in Cox's Bazar are frequently subjected to domestic violence. However, they are often unwilling and unable to seek help or register complaints. Domestic violence is acceptable in the Rohingya community to a certain extent and there is deep stigma attached to bringing out its instances in the public domain. Furthermore, there is insufficient access to and lack of information about services and authorities that they can approach for help. The men of the families usually act as gatekeepers and the Majhis (informal community leaders who are almost all men) very often control access to information and interface with authorities. This can create a hostile environment where women may feel trapped and are further isolated.

However, the solidarity women forge with other survivors of sexual assault in camps and settlements can sometimes help them in dealing with the trauma. Maoualmin shares, "What helped me during all those years is that there is a form of women's solidarity. It healed so many wounds."

Lalla, another West-Sahara refugee living in Haussa, told us that she was raped at gunpoint at the time of displacement. She met many women in the camp who were victims of sexual violence. The women all share their stories with each other in the hopes of comforting each other. The pain, however, always remains.

Family separation in exile

Family separation is a significant social, emotional, and financial burden for many refugees who have had to flee conflict.[8] It has also long been associated with increased psychological distress and physical health challenges.[9,10] It is common to encounter cases amongst refugees where family members have been separated in displacement. Family members may have been left behind in the country of origin, while a few have escaped and taken refuge elsewhere.

Living in Gleibet Lfoula camp, a West-Sahara refugee Maymouna says that her father enabled them to flee to safety during the war. She left with her mother, sisters, and brothers, one of whom was just a month old at that time. Her father, grandmother, and aunt could not escape with them.

Several of the refugees interviewed for this study are single women; they are either widows or separated from their husbands. In the case of displaced Rohingyas in Bangladesh, it is usual for the husbands and other male family members to have been either killed or detained in Myanmar. In many such cases, women have had to flee alone with their children.

Amina, a refugee living in the DRC, fled from Burundi in 2015 with her sister and their children. Her sister's husband had been killed by militia men, who then took Amina's husband away. Amina says that she has had no news of him since and is not sure whether he is alive or dead. In the chaos that ensued during their escape, Amina lost one of her children. She and the others tried to find the child for days but to no avail.

No one is prepared to flee, Amina says grimly. People could never imagine giving up their possessions, their livelihoods, and their homes and leaving until they are forced to do so.

Despite the concerted efforts of humanitarian actors in Bangladesh to support Rohingya women and girls since the mass forced displacement in 2017, grave concerns remain. Along with increasing reports of domestic and intimate partner violence, there is also an increasing number of cases of sexual harassment and SGBV against Rohingya women in general. Additionally, there is a high risk of trafficking of both women and girls.

These concerns regarding sexual harassment and trafficking are much more acute for women who are unmarried or considered to be single as they are widowed, divorced, separated, or abandoned. Women in the Rohingya camps have been sharing instances of their heightened vulnerability as their partners are missing or dead or have abandoned their families and have gone on to marry other women. These abandoned women are in a situation where they must manage their families alone without necessarily having the means required to do so. This can typically force them to enter abusive relationships or resort to precarious means of survival and to allow their children to work or marry their daughters off early.

The situation of single women and female-headed households is also worsened as they are unable to access relief and welfare services provided in host countries. This is especially the case if services are provided at the household level on the basis of existing documents or new registration such that it identifies only the male member as the head of the household, regardless of whether he is present anymore or not. Unseen and unheard in this manner, the effects of being separated from their families are compounded manifold for women in exile.

Invisibility in the host country

In all conflicts, women suffer in ways specific to women. Yet they should not be seen as a homogenous group; different women have different needs, vulnerabilities, and coping mechanisms. When relief and rehabilitation efforts do not recognise these differential needs, the deprivation and denial of basic rights that women face is further intensified.

It is well understood that SGBV tends to be exacerbated where family and community protection structures have broken down, as is frequently the case in displacement contexts and protracted crises. In refugee camps, women and girls who are living in crowded shelters, accessing latrines and bathing spaces at night or in bad lighting, and accessing crowded marketplaces, etc., are at high risk of SGBV. A large number of women report instances of sexual and psychological abuse in relief shelters and relief queues. Yet refugee campsites often come up or are set up in a manner which negates the safety and protection requirements of women and girls. Moreover, host country governments sometimes may not extend legal protection to refugees which makes it impossible for women to register formal complaints and seek justice in case they wish to do so. There might also be a lack of informal mechanisms in refugee camps that they can approach.

The movement of women and girls is usually restricted to the confines of refugee camps. They cannot work outside and do not have linkages to markets, inputs, and credit for setting up their own enterprise within the camps. In such scenarios, women refugees, especially those who are single, struggle to make ends meet and pay for education, healthcare, and other basic needs for their families. For women who live outside of camps, the situation may be even more dire. They may not be able to access any support services or aid at all and might also be excluded from the informal economy due to restrictive traditional norms within the community, restrictions placed by the host country authorities or the lack of jobs in safe working conditions. Further, they may not have access to essential healthcare and psychological counselling.

Safi is from Burundi and currently lives in Goma, DRC. With the support of a small livelihoods programme run by UNHCR, she was able to open a small business and pay for essential needs such as food and school fees. But as her children are growing up, her worries are increasing. She laments that the money she makes is not enough to cover their expenses, especially as their studies are becoming more expensive. She has very little savings and has been unable to invest back into the business and consolidate her earnings.

Similarly, Maymouna from West Sahara is struggling to meet her expenses. She says,

> Look at me. I have many health issues. I suffer from heart rhythm problems, thyroid disease, and breast cancer. I have to stay in the local health centre each time for months. My mom is also sick. It's my daughter who takes care of her. She has stopped her study at the university to look after her grandmother. We don't have hospitals (in the camp), this is why we have to travel for medical care. So, this is my life. I leave the camp to come here to the health centre and I go back to the camp. The difficult conditions of life in the camps make us sicker.

As a result, many refugees, especially older ones, share a sense of hopelessness at the endless waiting in camps and at the bleak opportunities that exist for their future generations to improve their lives. Refugees in protracted situations are especially susceptible to being marginalised and being forgotten by governments of the host countries or humanitarian organisations, with little recourse and support.

Jayapriya, a refugee from Sri Lanka living in India, says that her family has been receiving the same allowance and entitlements for years, but in the meantime their expenditure on rent, education, and other essential items has been increasing. At the same time, youngsters from the community with good education are unable to get decent jobs which are appropriate to their qualification and skills. It is even tougher for young women to find decent jobs.

The lives of the refugees are thus always full of struggles and uncertainties, and with little hope, says Jayapriya. She feels that they are constantly "othered" and treated as refugees wherever they go, and there is no integration or assimilation possible for them.

Safi also talks about the sense of alienation she feels. She says that though refugees live with local communities in Goma, there is a palpable lack of trust and tension among communities. The proliferation of armed groups in the region, including militias of Burundian origin has made matters worse. Safi says that refugees are constantly afraid of being targeted or being denied services. She is saddened by the lack of comfort and familiarity.

The common scenario of refugee camps and settlements across the world is full of countless faces of displaced people. They are at the receiving end of crippling poverty, deprivation, violence, and lack of identity. They lack access to fundamental services and their rights are routinely denied and trampled upon.

Yet the women continue to show incredible resilience. "You know, we are refugees and our parents taught us to be patient. We transmitted this value to our children. When you grow up in basic tents, you have to be patient," says Maymouna.

They often talk of their aspirations and hopes, most of which are centred around better lives for their children. In one of our interactions with women who fled Myanmar in 2017, Ayesha Bibi tells us,

> I would like to return to my country one day but with a written document that ensures my independence and rights. If we have to live in dire conditions in both the countries, I would rather live in Bangladesh. It ensures the safety of my children's lives at least. All I am doing now is thinking of how to ensure a brighter future for my children.

Conclusion

This chapter draws upon our experience as humanitarian workers responding to the Rohingya refugee crisis in Cox's Bazar. We have observed first-hand the protection challenges that women face in the camps. Their movement within the camps and their participation in decision-making spaces is highly controlled and restricted by men. In many cases, religious leaders have been known to restrict women and adolescent girls' mobility and access to safe spaces as well as public places. Polygamy is practiced in the camps, resulting in many cases of abandonment. Moreover, the restrictions on movement of the camp population have led to protection problems because high levels of inactivity have contributed to the rise of illegal activities such as substance abuse, gambling, sexual harassment and abuse, etc.

Single women and female heads of households are particularly vulnerable to sexual exploitation and abuse. Overcrowding and infrastructural deficiencies in the camps are increasing protection risks for women. For example, insufficient number of toilets often located at long distances from shelters are exposing women and girls to greater risk of sexual harassment and violence. Limited streetlights also make it harder for women to move freely in camps during the night. There are other socio-economic factors such as cultural traditions, insufficient humanitarian assistance, lack of formal education, healthcare and appropriate legal assistance, and limited income-generating possibilities, etc., that contribute to protection risks for women.

Despite the various challenges and constant tensions, women in the camps often self-organise and engage with different kinds of networks. These networks help them to deal with their pain and heal their wounds by sharing their experiences with each other. They also create supporting structures and safety nets based on the solidarity amongst them.

Protection and prevention strategies need to support this sense of agency by responding to women as "survivors", and not as "victims", and focusing on ensuring their rights and empowerment. There needs to be recognition of the fact that women and adolescent girls are the most vulnerable in any humanitarian crisis situation and when a crisis is particularly sexually violent and gendered, there is a greater need to ensure that women and adolescent girls take on leadership positions.

Our experience in establishing women's safe spaces in the Rohingya camps in Cox's Bazar has been an overwhelmingly positive one in this respect. These are spaces where only women and girls are allowed to enter and gather for various activities. Here women can process their trauma, be safe from violence, and plan for the future. At these centres, women and adolescent girls receive psychological first aid and individual counselling from trained counsellors so that they can deal with their psychological distress and obtain healthcare checks and referrals, including menstrual health services. They are also provided with information and awareness building on violence against women and girls and the risks of child marriage and support in reporting concerns. In addition, these centres offer women a chance to socialise, make friends, and support each other.

In 2018, in a group discussion, one of the participants shared her experience of coming to the safe space.

> We feel good when we come to *Shantikhana* (a peaceful place, referring to Women Safe Spaces). We talk with other women and girls and I forget everything. We have received dignity kits, lights to go to the toilet at night. If I face any problems, I come here to talk to these sisters. I feel good here. Whenever I go back to my shelter, all the bad memories come back to me.

Rohingya women have been gradually getting involved in various activities taking place in and around the women-friendly spaces. These activities include volunteering, education and skill training, community mobilisation, providing psycho-social support to other community women and meetings with local authorities (e.g. camp coordination meetings) and international authorities (e.g. foreign official delegations and representatives of international organisations), etc., to share their voices and demands.

These spaces, therefore, also serve as a hub to support Rohingya women's empowerment through confidence building. They have been instrumental in increasing women's community participation and in enabling them to take on leadership roles. Women now participate in equal numbers in Community Watch groups, Water, Sanitation and Hygiene (WASH) groups, etc., and take ownership of the various activities that they are involved in. They use the women-friendly spaces as a safe forum to discuss the issues and challenges that they might be facing from authorities and community members and collectively devise strategies to deal with them.

The safe spaces are also trying to be inclusive. Innovative programmes such as on-and off-air radio programmes are being arranged to reach out to the community, specially women with disabilities who cannot come to women's safe spaces. Volunteers working in the camps on cyclone preparedness and evacuation have been trained with a focus on vulnerable groups such as women and young children.

The basic education and skill development support that they receive at the safe spaces may also enable women and girls to be engaged in non-formal income generation, which helps in restoring their self-esteem and confidence.

Hence, while recognising women's rights as a non-negotiable agenda, it is imperative that humanitarian stakeholders and host country governments promote equal opportunities for women to ensure their participation at all levels. They must develop strategies and design programmes to include the most vulnerable and marginalised women, build on women's existing capacities, address barriers to women's leadership, strengthen women's access to resources, and create safe spaces for women and girls to organise and mobilise.

In order to achieve gender equality before and during a humanitarian crisis and to maximise the contribution of humanitarian responses, it is crucial to keep women and girls at the centre of planning. A gender-integrated approach that empowers women and girls and engages men and boys, is crucial for achieving long-term positive change, transforming deeply entrenched inequalities, and developing resilience.

Notes

1 See Lalla's interview in Chapter 3 of this book.
2 "The Effects of Armed Conflict on Girls and Women," November 18, 2009. Cited in https://www.tandfonline.com/doi/pdf/10.1207/s15327949pac0404_6. Accessed on May 15, 2019.
3 "This Is How it Feels to Be Lonely," Cited in https://migrantsorganise.org/wp-content/uploads/2014/09/Loneliness-report_The-Forum_UPDATED.pdf. Accessed on May 15, 2019.
4 "Bangladesh Refugee Emergency Population Factsheet," June 14, 2018. Cited in https://www.humanitarianresponse.info/sites/www.humanitarianresponse.info/files/documents/files/unhcrbangladesh_populationfactsheet_14june2018.pdf. Accessed on May 15, 2019.
5 The examples referred to in the chapter are from the narratives presented in Chapter 3 of this book, unless otherwise specified.
6 Zachary Steel et al., "Impact of Immigration Detention and Temporary Protection on the Mental Health of Refugees," *British Journal of Psychiatry*, 2006.
7 World Health Organization, *World Health Report 2001 – Mental Health: New Understanding, New Hope* (Switzerland: WHO, 2001).
8 "Refugee Family Reunification: UNHCR's Response to the European Commission Green Paper on the Right to Family Reunification of Third Country Nationals Living in the European Union (Directive 2003/86/ EC)," February 2012. Cited in https://www.unhcr.org/4f54e3fb13.pdf. Accessed on September 9, 2019.
9 Angela Nickerson et al., "The Familial Influence of Loss and Trauma on Refugee Mental Health: A Multilevel Path Analysis," *Journal of Traumatic Stress*, January 25, 2011.
10 Matthew R. Stevens, "The Collapse of Social Networks among Syrian Refugees in Urban Jordan," *Contemporary Levant*, April 16, 2016.

9
WOMEN, SOCIAL POSITIONING, AND REFUGEE STATUS

Rose Jaji

Introduction

When violent conflict erupts, many people stay on in their countries with the hope that the conflict will be contained before much damage is done. This does not usually turn out to be the case, as several violent conflicts around the world attest to. In many cases of political impasse, violence is resorted to as a quick "solution" but once it has started, it is difficult to quell. Countries that have experienced violent conflicts show that these more often than not tend to be long drawn-out, thus creating protracted refugee situations. The majority of the people in the affected area tend to flee only as a last resort because they hold on to the hope that the conflict will end before much harm is inflicted and many lives are lost. By the time the people who are affected realise the hopelessness of their circumstances, the security situation has deteriorated to the extent of making flight itself risky. Both women and men suffer during violent conflicts and experience gross human rights violations, but their experiences are gendered.

Insofar as contemporary conflicts have been transferred from the battlefield to civilian spaces, they claim many unarmed people's lives. Although very few women participate as combatants in armed conflicts around the world, they are often targeted in these conflicts.[1] In addition to maiming and violent deaths, women are also more vulnerable to sexual and gender-based violence. Women's challenges are compounded by the fact that in many cultures around the world, they are caregivers on whom other family members depend for nurturing and care, for example, children, the infirm and the elderly. A combination of women's low social position in many cultural contexts and refugee status engenders situations in which they are particularly vulnerable to not only physical insecurity but also material want.

DOI: 10.4324/9781003047094-9

Destruction of livelihoods that accompanies violent conflicts and persecution leaves affected women in conditions of extreme poverty and despair. Without timely and relevant interventions in countries of asylum, this situation creates a vicious circle that traps generations in circumstances characterised by marginalisation, perpetual suffering, and uncertainty. It is important to acknowledge and address women's suffering during conflicts, but interventions need to go beyond their victimhood and focus on their agency and resilience as part of the efforts to rebuild their lives. Adaptation to life in the country of asylum calls for programmes that enable refugee women to realise their dream of a secure life in both physical and economic terms.

The transience fallacy and host country fatigue

For the majority of refugees in the Global South, flight means exacerbation and transplantation of material deprivation from the country of origin to the country of asylum. For example, many host countries such as Kenya, Tanzania, Zambia, Jordan, and Bangladesh pursue encampment policies that contain refugees in spaces where they mostly rely on humanitarian assistance. There are refugees who live outside the camps in these countries but achieving self-sufficiency remains a challenge.[2] On account of the abruptness of flight in most cases, refugees generally arrive in the camps with very little to sustain themselves. This is particularly the case for people from poor backgrounds who flee their countries with very little if any resources to rebuild their livelihoods, for example, by starting small businesses.

Although there are numerous cases of protracted situations across the world, refugee policies continue to be premised on the view that refugees are a temporary phenomenon. Camps are accordingly designed as transient spaces where refugees are contained as they await repatriation. Where refugees are hosted in neighbouring countries, the camps are often located close to borders with the country of origin for easy repatriation and this arrangement exposes refugees to cross-border raids by armed militias from their countries of origin.[3] The idea of transience persists in refugee hosting notwithstanding evidence showing how refugee camps have become spaces of permanent waiting. Only a few countries such as Uganda host refugees in settlements where refugees are provided with land for agricultural activities.

In addition to the transience fallacy, the intractability of many conflicts around the world has led to host country fatigue observable in growing hostility towards refugees as they spend more time than anticipated in the country of asylum. Many conflicts persist such that refugees have not been able to repatriate as presumed under the encampment regime. The longer violent conflicts have taken to resolve, the more hostile host countries have become. In such cases, the refugees are increasingly perceived as agents rather than victims of insecurity. Many host countries such as Kenya and Tanzania that pursue the encampment policy see refugees as a burden. For example, in 2016, Kenya attempted to close Dadaab

Refugee Camp and forcibly repatriate Somali refugees. This course of action was, however, stopped by the High Court of Kenya which ruled in February 2017 that closing the camp was unconstitutional. Where refugees reside among citizens, they are increasingly associated with and blamed for crime, insecurity, and other social ills. The humanitarian assistance that they receive may generate resentment among locals living in conditions of material deprivation who do not appreciate their exclusion from the same assistance that is provided to refugees living in their communities. This resentment has sometimes degenerated into violence against refugees thus creating an additional layer of violence in their lives.[4]

Provision of land, vocational training, start-up capital, and other resources necessary for economic activities enables refugees to wean themselves from humanitarian assistance and this restores the dignity that they have lost through flight, abandonment of their means of livelihoods, and dependence on charity. For women, who have the primary responsibility of feeding children and other family members due to culturally defined gender roles,[5] access to land for agricultural activities enables them to take control of family consumption patterns and household nutritional requirements. Agricultural productivity enables refugee women to make decisions on what they feed their families which rarely happens in camps where refugees eat what they receive as food rations.

In a research that I conducted from September 2006 to February 2007 with refugees from the Great Lakes region living in Nairobi, Kenya, food rations that were unsuitable for household needs were one of the main reasons why the women left refugee camps and self-settled in the city where they could engage in income-generating activities and purchase food items they deemed appropriate for their households. The absence of arrangements for self-reliance such as those obtaining in Uganda's refugee settlements means that refugees continue to depend on humanitarian assistance for as long as they reside in the camps.

In cases where refugees are allowed to settle among citizens, many face obstacles because of lack of identity documents and inability to obtain necessary documents such as work permits that would enable them to seek employment and gain access to opportunities that are available to citizens. Many refugees live in a state of "included exclusion"[6] characterised by lack of citizenship or other forms of formal recognition such as protection letters that would enable them to rebuild their lives in the country of asylum. Lack of the necessary documents and opportunities in the country of asylum affects both educated as well as uneducated refugees. This means that the refugee status has a homogenising effect on people who flee violent conflicts, persecution, and gross human rights violations regardless of their differential socio-economic backgrounds because without necessary documents, even refugees who possess specific skills are unable to seek employment. Asylum seekers from economically stable backgrounds often leave behind their material possessions and arrive with almost as little as those who were poor in the country of their origin. Where refugees from wealthier backgrounds may arrive with savings or money obtained from selling their valuables, they will eventually need to seek sustainable ways of earning a living. Whether they decide to seek employment or start businesses, they still need relevant documents.

Refugee women and the difficulties they face

Cultural and religious beliefs that deny girls and women formal education persist in many parts of the Global South. Girls who are denied education are most likely to be economically and socially disempowered and dependent on men who may be their fathers, brothers, and husbands. This state of perpetual dependence places women in a precarious position, which exposes them to abuse especially by men as intimate partners. Economic dependence curtails women's decision-making capacity, freedom of choice, and self-determination. One of the challenges that refugee women face is conformity to gender norms in restrictive circumstances. These norms include deference to men who are no longer in a position to perform normative masculinity, and effective mothering in severely constrained economic circumstances. Poverty has a detrimental effect on performance of normative femininity built around motherhood as many cases of refugee women living under conditions of extreme material deprivation demonstrate.

However, many women strive to be economically independent but without much or any education and professional training, most of them have limited access to economic opportunities in the formal sector where incomes are typically more predictable, stable, and reliable. The majority of women without formal education and training are thus confined to the informal sector where incomes are unstable and inadequate. Most of the economic activities such as domestic work and selling food in the informal sector available to women with limited or no education and professional training generate low incomes that allow women to meet only the bare minimum of household consumption needs. The circumstances of many poor women in the Global South illustrate the mutually reinforcing relationship between lack of education and abject poverty. This creates a vicious cycle in the sense that without education, many women remain trapped in extreme poverty and in turn children, especially girls, born into poor families, lack access to education and are unable to break the cycle of poverty.

Women's situation is exacerbated by the fact that sometimes violent conflicts claim their husbands' lives and leave them and their children relying on a single and inadequate income from informal economic activities. In cultures where women are not allowed or encouraged to work outside the home, adjusting to the new reality of earning an income outside the home as a widow makes life even more difficult. Flight does not necessarily alleviate the plight of women because it means that the women have to find ways of sustaining their families in a foreign country whose legal requirements for or reluctance to grant citizenship or naturalisation and the right to seek employment usually compound the challenges that they face. This is particularly difficult for women because they usually flee with dependent family members.

Even in situations where women flee with their husbands, this does not guarantee them physical and economic security. In most cases, women bear the brunt of troubled masculinities that emanate from men's inability to fulfil culturally defined gender roles, frustration, and aggression. A combination of trauma and frustration over inability to provide for the family results in refugee men perpetrating domestic violence on their wives.[7] When failure to play the breadwinner's role takes its toll on men, the result is that they either commit suicide or abandon the family, leaving women to shoulder a double burden.

Insofar as violent conflicts take their toll on civilians, women's bodies have become the battleground upon which deviant and violent masculinities define and stamp their hegemony. Many women not only have to deal with the pain of losing family members and means of livelihoods but also with vulnerability to sexual and gender-based violence. Refugee women's stories are oftentimes stories of gross sexual abuse and misogyny perpetrated by men in their families and communities as well as men from hostile communities in the name of ethnic cleansing. Men from hostile communities or armed militias and combatants also regard violation of women as a way of emasculating men from the women's families and communities at large.

For women who get caught up in violent conflicts, there is a fine line between the joys and sorrows of motherhood. Sometimes women watch helplessly as their daughters are violated and taken away against their will and they have had to put their own lives at risk in order to protect their daughters or prioritise their children's welfare. There are many instances in which such concerns are well founded, especially in cases where women from marginalised and persecuted groups are treated as possessions and their families are unable to seek redress because of intimidation by the perpetrators and indifference by the authorities.

Insecurity remains a serious problem for women not only in their homes when they are attacked but also during and after flight.[8] Flight does not necessarily mean safety and security because it may signal the beginning of other forms of violations from a new group of perpetrators who may be fellow inmates of the refugee camp or citizens of the country of asylum. Although refugee camps conform to the design of total institutions in terms of administrative and physical separation from the outside world,[9] refugee women who reside in them remain vulnerable to violence and insecurity. In African refugee camps, refugee women are known to be targeted and raped when they leave their shelters in order to fetch firewood from the forest, for example. In situations where refugees from different national and cultural backgrounds are housed together, the women may be exposed to sexual abuse by men who may not necessarily accord them the same respect they give to women from their own communities.

Similarly, insecurity outside the country of origin means that many women live with a lot of anxiety because of concerns about their security and that of their children especially their daughters who face the same sexual and gender-based violence. Even in the confines of the camps, unmarried women who do not have male family members to protect them are targeted for sexual harassment.

The irony is that many women seek to avert sexual harassment by attaching themselves to men and this sometimes exposes them to even more grievous sexual and gender-based violence. Sometimes, in a cruel twist, the same men who flee violence together with women morph into perpetrators in many camp environments thus rendering women vulnerable even in the country of asylum. The general insecurity that unmarried women experience can force them into marriage for physical, social, and cultural security which can lead to more physical and sexual violence by men as husbands thus compounding the women's suffering.

Vulnerability to physical violence by partners and other family members or community members persists in the host country due to various assumptions by host governments, policy makers and aid workers about family life and gender relations obtaining therein. Firstly, there is the assumption that male family members protect women. This presupposition emanates from construction of the family as a haven of safety and protection. The second assumption that follows from the first is that women and girls are abused by non-kin men. Lastly, there is the assumption that women accept continued existence under patriarchal surveillance because it is "their culture." In the context of refugee camps, these assumptions are illustrated by territorialisation of accommodation by which refugees from the same country live in the same zone of the camp. In urban centres, refugees from the same countries or cultural backgrounds are normally accommodated in the same shelters and apartment blocks, which usually exposes women to moral policing by men from their families and communities. There have been cases of women who escaped armed conflict only to die in the host country at the hands of male family members in the name of family honour or hostile non-kin men.

Exile and opportunities

Whereas flight entails loss in its various forms, it sometimes presents opportunities and organisations that assist refugees in general, and women in particular need to seize them. In countries of origin, women may conform to social organisation and relations rooted in culture and religion. Numerous women have lived under the patriarchal gaze, the main consequence of which has been the stifling of their aspirations and non-realisation of their full potential. Against this background, flight presents opportunities for refugee women to resist patriarchal control because it may provide physical and social space to women to evade unfavourable cultural practices such as forced and arranged marriages, female circumcision, widow inheritance, and economic dependence on men. However, despite the huge strides that have been made to address women's interests and protect them in cases of gender conflicts in a significant number of countries in the Global South, deeply entrenched cultural and religious norms remain intact in some countries such that women rarely have any recourse in cases where they need legal protection.

There is a possibility for positive change where appropriate structures are put in place in the country of asylum to redress the situation of refugee women from such backgrounds. In the research with refugees in Nairobi, refugee women took advantage of living in a foreign country to challenge unfavourable cultural practices such as female circumcision, arranged marriages, and staying on in marriages where the husband was unfaithful. For example, they would appeal to NGOs to assist them in cases of marital disputes. The NGOs offered the necessary emotional, moral, and legal support which the women did not receive from family members and community elders in both countries of origin and the new communities established in the country of asylum. Unmarried refugee women also resisted control by family members especially the elders by moving away from communities where their compatriots clustered and living on their own in neighbourhoods where they could exercise freedom of choice without older women's interference and admonition.[10] For example, some young Muslim women in Nairobi relocated to neighbourhoods where the refugee population was predominantly Christian.[11] In these cases, flight and mobility within the country of asylum are a form of spatial resistance to the patriarchal gaze trained especially on young women by older women and male community elders.

Relocation to countries with different political and socio-cultural organisations may also enable women to end abusive marriages and find legal support from various organisations and the judicial system where they have been formally granted refugee status. For example, Sudanese women resettled in the United States took advantage of the legal protection provided to women by their host country to divorce and evade the censure that their choices would have entailed in their country of origin.[12]

In host countries where women's rights are promoted and protected, therefore, there are opportunities for women to engage in cultural introspection and adopt new values and use them to raise their status through, for example, quest for education, employment, and other opportunities that they were denied in the country of origin for various socio-cultural and economic reasons. Cultural and legal contexts that promote women's rights offer space for autonomy. As such, when women flee war, this can also be a case of flight from oppressive socio-cultural practices that marginalise and disempower them and an opportunity to obtain freedoms denied them thus far.

Quest for self-reliance

The stereotypical depiction of refugee women as helpless victims persists, and it has fed into policies that are designed with little, if any, input by the women. While it is true that many refugee women have suffered some of the worst forms of abuse and human rights violations, it is important to avoid reducing them to perpetual victims, incapable of helping themselves. Notwithstanding the suffering and abuse that refugee women endure, most of them are resilient and they seek to rebuild their lives and those of their children or other dependent family members. This requires appropriate interventions such as psychological and material support, especially at the beginning. Healing from trauma requires as much effort as possible towards normalisation of life outside the country of origin through fostering of self-reliance.

Violent conflict affects people from various educational and socio-economic backgrounds, which means that the category of refugee women is heterogenous. There are women among the refugees who are capable of making a contribution not only to their own welfare but also to the host country contrary to the stereotype that refugees are helpless and dependent. Many refugee women do not want to become perpetual dependents on humanitarian assistance, which means that opportunities should be created to simultaneously harness their skills for the benefit of the host country and reduce their dependence on humanitarian aid. For instance, providing professional refugee women with the necessary documents for them to use their skills would lift them out of the poverty that flight entails. Many host countries in Africa are grappling with the brain drain caused by the migration of professionals. Providing the opportunity for refugees to work would fill the gap created by emigration from the host country.

Conclusion

Perception of refugees as a passing phenomenon has left many refugees in protracted situations in a state of limbo. This has a detrimental effect on refugee women, especially as their lives are intricately linked to those of their children and other dependent family members. It is the women who are responsible for household consumption needs, and refugee assistance programmes need to be cognisant of this fact and respond in a manner which enhances women's self-reliance and autonomy in exile.

The plight of many refugee women can be traced back to the country of origin. The disempowering socio-economic and political conditions that refugee women may have faced in the country of origin can also have debilitating impacts in exile. Denial of education to girls constitutes a severe economic handicap in their adulthood which can have an impact for the rest of their lives, for example. Many women who lack formal education and training mostly rely on men as husbands and/or eke out a living on the economic margins of their societies. Once they have become mothers, the women who as girls were denied the resources and opportunities to pursue their dreams, generally transfer these dreams and aspirations on to their children, especially their daughters; but in the context of flight and life as a refugee, the dire economic straits that the women live in are an obstacle to their wish to provide decent education to their children. A vicious circle is thus created in which refugee women's children are unable to lift themselves and their own families out of poverty.

There is also a need to open the cultural door to refugee women and enable them to speak out and make their preferences and choices known in terms of residential arrangements as some of them may prefer not to live under patriarchal surveillance and censure. Many refugee women may find that exile provides them the opportunity to rebuild a new life, and interventions to assist them should focus more on enabling them to become self-reliant and educate their children so that the cycle of poverty can be broken. Self-sufficiency is an important aspect of adaptation to life in the host country and long-term healing and post-flight restoration.

Notes

1 Human Rights Watch, *Women and Armed Conflict* (New York: Human Rights Watch, 2012).
2 Rose Jaji, "Social Technology and Refugee Encampment in Kenya," *Journal of Refugee Studies* Vol. 25, No. 2: 2011, pp. 221–238; Sarah Zayed, "Self Sufficiency in Refugees," *Independent Study Project (ISP) Collection*. 2477, 2016.
3 Rose Jaji, "Social Technology and Refugee Encampment in Kenya," *Journal of Refugee Studies* Vol. 25, No. 2: 2011, pp. 221–238.
4 Sebastian Jäckle and Pascal D. König, "Threatening Events and Anti-Refugee Violence: An Empirical Analysis in the Wake of the Refugee Crisis during the Years 2015 and 2016 in Germany," *European Sociological Review*, Vol. 34, No. 6: 2018, pp. 728–743; Rose Jaji, *Refugee Women and the Experiences of Local Integration in Nairobi, Kenya*, PhD thesis, Bayreuth University, Germany, 2009.
5 Caroline O. N. Moser, *Gender Planning and Development Theory, Practice and Training* (London: Routledge, 1993).
6 Simon Turner, 2006. "Biopolitics and Bare Life in a Refugee Camp Some Conceptual Reflections," in Katharina Inhetveen, Hg., *Flucht als Politik Berichte von fünf Kontinenten* (Köln: RüdigerKöppe Verlag, 2006), pp. 39–62.
7 Jane Freedman, "Sexual and Gender-based Violence against Refugee Women: A Hidden Aspect of the Refugee 'Crisis,'" *Reproductive Health Matters* Vol. 24, No. 47: 2016, pp. 18–26.
8 Jane Freedman, "Sexual and Gender-Based Violence against Refugee Women: A Hidden Aspect of the Refugee 'Crisis,'" *Reproductive Health Matters* Vol. 24, No. 47: 2016, pp. 18–26; Amy R. Friedman, "Rape and Domestic Violence," *Women and Therapy* Vol. 13, No. 1-2: 1992, pp. 65–78.
9 Susan Forbes Martin, *Refugee Women* (Lanham: Lexington Books, 2004).
10 See Patricia Ehrkamp, "'I've Had It with Them!' Younger Migrant Women's Spatial Practices of Conformity and Resistance," *Gender, Place and Culture* Vol. 20, No. 1: 2013, pp. 19–36; Rose Jaji, "Normative, Agitated, and Rebellious Femininities among East and Central African Refugee Women," *Gender, Place and Culture* Vol. 22, No. 4: 2015, pp. 494–509.
11 Rose Jaji, "Normative, Agitated, and Rebellious Femininities among East and Central African Refugee Women," *Gender, Place and Culture* Vol. 22, No. 4: 2015, pp. 494–509.
12 Dianna J. Shandy, *Nuer Passages Globalizing Sudanese Migration* (Gainesville, FL: University Press of Florida, 2007).

10
FORCED MIGRATION AND THE GENDERING OF SURVIVAL IN EXILE

Romola Sanyal

Forced migrants are amongst the most vulnerable people in the world. This vulnerability stems not only from their situation wherein they are forcibly displaced from their homes and their home countries, but also because their legal status leaves them with little protection and safeguards in their host countries and communities. As crises become protracted, this legal vulnerability also becomes more serious for refugees and their families. This chapter offers a look at some of the ways in which the situation of forced migrants becomes more precarious in exile, how they cope in these situations and how the precarity itself is inherently gendered.

Introduction

The world is witnessing the largest forced displacement of people in history and this trend is set to become worse, with no amelioration in sight. As groups and communities of people around the world move for a variety of intertwining reasons – poverty, conflict, environmental crises – what futures can these displaced people anticipate in countries and spaces where in which they are hosted? Unfortunately, although people are fleeing from dire circumstances, leaving behind all that is familiar and all that was home for unknown shores, their reception in receiving countries is rather mixed. Indeed, many societies are sympathetic to their plight, particularly towards forced migrants who are escaping from conflict and persecution, but such sympathy is often short-lived or is at least affected by the difficult economic, political, and environmental circumstances that host communities themselves may be facing. Protracted displacement, which is becoming the norm, puts considerable pressure on local resources and infrastructure, and ultimately hospitality and relations can shift over time.[1]

DOI: 10.4324/9781003047094-10

In the case of forced migrants, one tool that has long been used to separate refugees from local communities and purportedly alleviate possible tensions between them is the use of refugee camps, particularly in countries in the Global South.[2] These camps can hold hundreds of thousands of people and exist for many decades, especially as crises become protracted. Here forced migrants are largely dependent on aid to keep them alive, and economic activities and the potential to earn a reasonable living from them are often limited.[3] However, while this model has been active for many years, the trend has been for refugees to move into cities where they can pursue livelihoods, access healthcare, education, and other services that may be limited in camps.[4] In cities, or indeed in any non-camp location, forced migrants can be particularly vulnerable, especially if they do not have legal status to live in the country. And even if they have secured refugee status, there are often limits to how they can access services such as education, employment opportunities, or other kinds of rights. As a result, they are vulnerable to various forms of exploitation and harassment, leading them to live lives that are precarious and often impoverished. Refugees are often compelled to engage in informal activities in order to survive. Such activities can also be deeply gendered, and indeed taking an intersectional lens to understanding precariousness amongst forced migrants is an important way of unpacking the political economy of refuge.

In the next sections I discuss how poverty and vulnerability affect forced migrants and the kinds of coping mechanisms they utilise in order to survive. As part of this discussion, I engage with an examination of informal practices and how these can offer opportunities for forced migrants on the one hand but can also limit their ability to improve their living conditions on the other. Throughout these analyses, I take a gendered lens, using it to unpack how refugees access services such as education and gainful employment. Finally, in embarking on this journey I hope to show how such conditions are not the exception, but the norm and what is needed now perhaps more than ever is a more humane world in which refugees are seen as humans first and then as people. We must, as we face uncertain futures, seriously reconsider the political economy of hospitality and think about new ways of forging solidarity with some of the most vulnerable people in the world.

Precarious lives: poverty and informality as key features of forced displacement

Not all forced migrants are poor, albeit a very large number of them have to leave most of their assets, livelihoods, and homes as they escape conflict and persecution and make their way into host communities. The journeys they take can also exhaust the resources they have, and they may arrive with little or nothing in the host countries. Poverty then often already marks the start of their new lives as refugees. As Rahema who escaped from Myanmar into Bangladesh, Ruth who escaped from Uganda first to Tanzania and later to DRC, or Khushboo who left from Pakistan to go to India, show in their narratives, they arrived with little or nothing and either went into camps or into cities and other places to eke out a living. Aid agencies and host governments may or may not provide support for them, but this support may also be quite meagre – just enough for mere survival. Support for "crises" is temporal and subject to the vicissitudes of global conflicts and emergencies that move around the world. Thus, as new emergencies arise, funding for others becomes depleted. Alongside that are the concerns with providing for refugees in countries that are themselves quite poor. Such support is not only financially difficult, but also politically fraught as I discuss below. Unfortunately, as current trends indicate, crises are becoming more protracted and under these circumstances forced migrants may find themselves living in host countries for years, perhaps decades. Being dependent on aid is neither economically nor psychologically sustainable. What options do they have then to rebuild their lives and to enable alternate, more promising futures for themselves and for their families?

The opportunities that forced migrants have in host countries are very much contingent on what they are legally allowed to do, and also what host communities permit them to do. I tease these out in turn. The term forced migrant encompasses a broad range of people from refugees, to stateless persons, internally displaced persons, and others. These different categories of people also have different legal rights in different countries, which are also affected by constantly shifting geopolitics. Refugees are "protected" under the 1951 Refugee Convention and the 1967 Refugee Protocol. These agreements define refugees primarily as individuals fleeing persecution. They do not offer protection for other forms of involuntary migration including war, and generalised aggression towards large numbers of people. Regional conventions in some parts of the world do provide protection to such cases of mass displacement. The Cartagena Convention and the AU Convention are good examples of such agreements. In other regions such as Asia where significant refugee flows have and continue to occur, no such regional agreements exist. Furthermore, in many countries in the Middle East, South and South East Asia, there are no national legislations for recognition or treatment of refugees. These include countries such as Lebanon, Jordan, India, Malaysia, and Thailand, amongst others. People fleeing to these countries are classified in different ways depending on the geopolitical strategies of the host country. In many cases, they are referred to as migrants or displaced persons, not as refugees. Sometimes they are given de-facto refugee status, but none of these provide legal protection and therefore refugees are subject to harassment on a regular basis.[5] Even in countries that are signatories to the Refugee Convention, the rights of most forced migrants may be limited – legally and socially, thus affecting their ability to access services and opportunities such as education and employment. Refugees, for example, are often not allowed to engage in paid labour in their host countries, and if they are, this may be confined to the space of the camp itself. We see the consequences of this in the case with the Rohingya camps in Bangladesh. As Rahima notes in her story from

Bangladesh, it is possible for men and women to work inside the camp and earn some money, so several women do so by cultivating and selling vegetables, rearing chickens, sewing clothes, nets, and, in some cases, doing piece work such as sewing shoes. However, they are not allowed to sell their items outside so their ability to earn a decent livelihood is limited.

It is not just the camp space that places restrictions on how one is able to earn a livelihood, but, as noted above, also the legal status itself that limits possibilities. Research has shown how in countries where refugee status is not recognised, forced migrants are faced with various forms of regular harassment by both local communities and the authorities. For example, Kate Coddington's work on Thailand looks at how the country labels refugees as migrants and this lack of a protected status means that refugees have to regularly bribe people including the police with whatever little money they get from UNHCR.[6] They are also compelled to work in the informal sector in unstable and often hazardous employment. We can take this example to reflect on Jensy and Padma Jothi's narratives as Sri Lankan refugees and Khushboo and Suman Devi's narratives as stateless people from Pakistan into India. These examples show that the lack of rights profoundly affects how people are able to rebuild their lives in exile. Jensy and Padma Jothi talk about how having refugee status means that they are not considered for public sector jobs and have difficulty in getting jobs in the private sector even if they have good educational backgrounds. This particularly affects the youth who feel frustrated that despite being well qualified, they are shut out of certain forms of employment and are compelled to take up casual work in the informal sector for low wages. Khushboo and Suman Devi reflect on how their lack of citizenship in India has translated into their inability to get decent jobs and be able to secure more promising futures. As a result, they too are forced to take up informal work in order to make ends meet and struggle with poverty as they attempt to rebuild their lives and homes.

As I have noted above, it is not just the legal status that impacts people's abilities to access jobs, but also the attitudes of the local communities. Refugees often have to navigate a complex landscape of xenophobia, harassment, and discrimination.[7] Private employers may not want to hire refugees as Jensy noted. The local communities may also discriminate against them as was the case with Devi who found it difficult to secure accommodation because of her family's caste background. Similarly, Malaika, a refugee in Goma, had made considerable efforts to integrate into the local community, but prejudices against Rwandan refugees persisted in the DRC, making her feel discriminated against. These prejudices arose because of Rwandan rebels' atrocities against the Congolese in certain parts of the country. In other parts of the world as well, refugees face different kinds of restrictions on their ability to work. For example, in Lebanon, many municipalities have limited the opportunities for Syrian refugees to work, making their economic situation particularly precarious as they struggle to make ends meet.[8] Such restrictions mean that refugees find it increasingly difficult to escape enduring poverty in their spaces of exile, and what they might face in many cases is increasing poverty and in fact destitution.

Education plays a complex role in the alleviation of poverty. As Sarah Dryden-Peterson notes, there is a need to "conceptualize refugee education so that it can meet goals of cognitive mobility that accompany long-term uncertainty."[9] The ability to go to school and gain skills and knowledge is perceived to play an important part in securing more financially stable and dignified futures. However, forced migrants face a number of hurdles in terms of both accessing education and putting that to use. In some cases, displacement may disrupt educational trajectories. Suman Devi's daughter, for example, was unable to pursue an engineering degree as she had hoped and this led to tragic circumstances where she took her own life. In other cases, such as with the Tamil refugees in India, despite having good education, refugees are unable to find gainful employment and are thus compelled to work in jobs that are far below their skills. In other words, the poverty and deskilling that they face are structural and enforced as a result of restrictive environments in which their rights are limited. The implications of this on the youth in particular are significant,[10] yet the politics around this remains fraught with uncertainty and distress.[11]

Like for many other poorer populations, particularly in the Global South, informal work thus provides an important means of earning livelihoods for refugees. Scholars have discussed the merits and limitations of the informal sector for some time. For the purposes of this chapter I focus only on what it means for forced migrants to engage in the informal labour market. On the one hand, it offers possibilities of finding employment and being able to survive through exile. This is important as families and individuals need to make ends meet in difficult circumstances, in countries and regions that are facing issues of poverty and limited resources, and in the face of uncertainty about their futures. Not knowing if they will remain in their host countries and for how long makes uncertainty a fundamental part of everyday living. Informality offers the opportunity to construct a life in the present moment, however tenuous, in these difficult circumstances.

On the other hand, informality also limits opportunities for people, offering them few, if any, ways out of poverty, especially when coupled with their tenuous legal status. It becomes a mechanism of survival in most cases and in doing so it simply becomes a way of moving from one day to the next. In cases where refugees may be well-qualified to move beyond precarious, piece-meal and unprotected labour, being compelled to engage in informal work can not only be financially debilitating, but also psychologically destructive as it offers no meaningful future and opportunities for upward mobility. Again, it is important to consider here that informality is thrust upon forced migrants as a result of their legal status, and that unlike citizens of a country, they may not find a way to escape it. Informality thus becomes a form of containing people's activities and their futures rather than being an emancipatory force.[12]

The gendered nature of work

A key feature of the narratives presented is the inherently gendered nature of displacement, work, and survival in exile. In the previous section I focused on looking at the insecure nature of work and brought in the discussion of informal labour. In this section I make observations on its gendered nature.

Displacement is itself a gendered process and has effects on gender relations. As with other forms of migration, it is not possible to predict how in fact these may unravel.[13] However, as we look at forced migration, particularly at the narratives presented and place them against other examples of forced migration, we see that once again, the precarious status of people, the limited ability for them to return or resettle – all affect their social and economic positions in gendered ways. Women have unique challenges as forced migrants. They are often subjected to varying forms of sexual harassment, exploitation, and violence. They also access education, labour, and other services in ways that are informed by societal notions of the role of women. As Doreen Indra notes, refugee women "often lack the class and cultural resources to make their concerns heard, and they are constrained from protesting by both traditional gender roles and by altruistic considerations of the marginal psychological statuses of their men."[14] The ways in which women are inserted into the labour market are cases in point. As the narratives demonstrate, women either find it hard to access paid work, or, the jobs that they do are what one would label "women's work" which includes activities such as maid work, sewing, piece work, and so forth. Jensy for example, talks about how employment opportunities are few for women and more accessible to men. Bintou from a refugee camp in Ausserd also echoes the point that it is hard for women to find jobs. Jensy notes that women refugees are largely homebound or do odd jobs to support their families. Women who are qualified as tailors or nurses work as domestic workers. In many of the other narratives, women work in very specific jobs – mostly in sewing/tailoring and doing piece work such as making blouses, working as beauticians, and so forth. In other words, the work that refugees do is highly casualised, but within that, the work that women are able to access is particularly gendered and more precarious.

There has been considerable writing on the ways in which women's work is devalued, not only in terms of its worth, but also in terms of the remuneration it fetches. As mentioned earlier, on account of their rather tenuous legal status, refugees are subjected to various forms of abuse and exploitation. In many cases, refugees get paid less than others because of their vulnerable situation. In some cases, women refugees who may not otherwise have worked are also compelled to start working in order to make ends meet, or in case the security conditions in the host country make it difficult for men to work. In Lebanon for example, it is difficult for Syrian refugees to survive because many have not renewed their paperwork and have thus become illegal in the country. As the country has various checkpoints where men (largely) are often stopped and questioned, their mobility is highly constrained. As a result, women and children have to go out and work in order to survive and they often get paid lower wages than what men would earn for the same work. This has significant implications for men whose role as the traditional breadwinner is eroded, for women who face issues of safety and exploitation and for children who may have to drop out of school in order to work, jeopardising not only their safety, but also their future. The entire system of discrimination against refugees and refugee men in particular puts increased pressure on women and children and on the family structure more generally.[15]

On the other hand, this same issue of compelling women to go out to work may also work in the opposite direction. In my own work with refugee women living in Kolkata who came during the partition, it was evident that many of them were also pushed into working in order to make ends meet. Women entered a number of different professions including secretarial and administrative work, teaching, and so forth.[16] In many of the interviews, women felt tremendous pride in their accomplishments as working women. But there is a particular class element to this, as many of these women came from middle-class backgrounds. Further, even though they joined the workforce, a pattern emerges in that there are only specific professions that are considered appropriate for women. Such works which are predominantly middle, white-collar jobs do not provide substantial, if any, opportunities for women to reach positions of power.

In discussing the above, it is then important to pay attention to men as we untangle the discussions of gendered labour within refugee populations. What kinds of work can men do and how is their labour also feminised? By discussing the feminisation of labour here, I signal the "shift in gender relations toward those considered 'female' or feminine."[17] In other words, the work that men are compelled to do is seen to either be "women's work," or work that, rather than being more formal, secure, and well-paid, which traditionally allowed men to be the breadwinners of the family, has increasingly become informal, flexible, and precarious.[18] This new form of work that is more precarious and "feminised" undermines the financial and gendered authority of men in their households and elsewhere. Here, it becomes useful to pay attention to whether men are able to access work at all, and the kinds of work that men are able to do and how they see work as affecting their future. As the narratives from Jensy and Padma Jothi point out, men who may be well-qualified to do white-collar jobs find themselves only being able to access work in the informal sector, on a casual and informal basis because of their refugee status of lack of citizenship. Khushboo's narrative is even more devastating as she notes the death of her brother and the disappearance of her husband – both prompted by the inability to pay off debts, again driven by their lack of citizenship. Forced migration thus acts as a force of emasculation that erodes the role of men as the breadwinner and the protector of the family. It functions as a system of oppression, even within exile and limits the ability of people to "live" everyday lives in a dignified manner. Instead, it perpetuates new forms of violence.

Conclusion

We exist in an era that is witnessing increased forced migration, and greater securitisation of borders, which seeks to stop those looking for refuge. It is useful here to pose the question: When do we stop looking at people as refugees and see them instead as humans and specifically as men and women who face differing forms of structural violence both as a result of displacement, as well as in the process of relief and resettlement?[19] What does our continued insistence on viewing them as forced migrants do to erase their unique identities and therefore their positions and needs within family and societal structures? How does this affect their ability to craft lives, hopes, dreams, and futures whilst in exile? The narratives from forced migrants highlight the ways in which the labels that are assigned to them define particular presents and futures that tend to be impoverished and precarious. Even more troubling is the palpable sense that there appears to be little hope for the future. The processes of displacement, relief, and resettlement not only label people in specific ways that limit the rights that they are able to access, but also condition the ways in which local communities respond to them. This is not to suggest that forced migrants face the same situations everywhere, but that largely, there is a pattern of increasing securitisation and hostility towards forced migrants that translates into a narrowing space of protection and support for them.

Crafting a life in exile is thus fraught with difficulties and the possibility of creating futures amongst forced migrants is liminal and uncertain.[20] What we are doing is effectively punishing people for seeking protection for too long and this should be given a pause. It is necessary to ask ourselves why matters have evolved to this point and how our anxieties about our borders and imagined communities of nations translate into systemic oppression of some of the world's most vulnerable people. In doing so, it is also useful to pay attention to how such practices of securitisation and othering produce and entrench gender relations amongst the displaced and how that leads to the silencing and marginalisation of women and men in different ways and the restructuring of social and familial relations in problematic ways.

Forced migrants have much to contribute to their host societies and collectively there are myriad ways in which futures can be created that are sustainable for everyone. For example, forced migrants are often made scapegoats for larger developmental and security concerns. Rather than invest in infrastructural upgrading, improvement of socio-economic opportunities, education, and healthcare, amongst others, host governments pass the blame onto forced migrants for taking away jobs or putting pressure on infrastructure.[21] Whilst there is no doubt that mass displacement is disruptive and can cause stress in the refugee-saturated areas, donors and aid agencies can work with local and regional governments to create policies that can benefit everyone. Such policies are being pursued for example by some humanitarian organizations that have begun to implement area-based approaches, particularly in urban centers to benefit both refugees and hosts.[22] Governments that host the majority of the world's displaced people are quite poor themselves. The international community could take heed of that and provide means by which countries could address their own developmental needs whilst undertaking such a significant burden. There is need for caution here though as humanitarian aid is often used as a way to keep refugees and displaced persons away from the shores of wealthy nations which is deeply problematic. The global burden-sharing is highly uneven, to put it mildly, and countries in the Global North must do more to take on their share of the matter. Finally, civil society has an important role to play in all this. NGOs, media, human rights groups have played key roles in affecting the overall discourse towards refugees in positive and negative ways. Organizations can work towards creating more supportive narratives and environments and more welcoming spaces for forced migrants. It would help to not only create more compassion among people, but also enable the ability for both groups to thrive together. At a time when forced migration is only set to increase, we would do well to abandon punitive and discriminatory measures against forced migrants and be more inclusive as societies.

Notes

1. Cathrine Brun, "Hospitality: becoming 'IDPs' and 'hosts' in protracted displacement." *Journal of Refugee Studies* 23.3 (2010): 337–355; Loren B. Landau, "Beyond the losers: transforming governmental practice in refugee-affected Tanzania." *Journal of Refugee Studies* 16.1 (2003): 19–43.
2. Richard Black, "Putting refugees in camps." *Forced Migration Review* 2, August (1998): 4–7.
3. Awa M. Abdi, "In Limbo: Dependency, insecurity, and identity amongst Somali Refugees in Dadaab camps." *Refuge: Canada's Journal on Refugees* 22.2 (2005): 6–14; Gaim Kibreab, "The myth of dependency among camp refugees in Somalia 1979–1989." *Journal of Refugee Studies* 6.4 (1993): 321–349.
4. Jonathan Darling. "Forced migration and the city: irregularity, informality, and the politics of presence." *Progress in Human Geography* 41.2 (2017): 178–198; Caroline Wanjiku Kihato, and Loren B. Landau, "Stealth humanitarianism: negotiating politics, precarity and performance management in protecting the urban displaced." *Journal of Refugee Studies* 30.3 (2016): 407–425.; Karen Jacobsen, "Refugees and asylum seekers in urban areas: a livelihoods perspective." *Journal of Refugee Studies* 19.3 (2006): 273–286.
5. Kate Coddington, "Landscapes of refugee protection." *Transactions of the Institute of British Geographers* 43.3 (2018): 326–340; Pei Palmgren, "Navigating a hostile terrain: Refugees and human rights in southeast Asia." *Sociology Compass* 5.5 (2011): 323–335., Romola Sanyal, "Managing through ad hoc measures: Syrian refugees and the politics of waiting in Lebanon." *Political Geography* 66 (2018): 67–75.
6. Kate Coddington, (2018).
7. Karen Jacobsen, (2006).
8. Romola Sanyal, (2018).
9. Sarah Dryden-Peterson, "Refugee education: education for an unknowable future." *Curriculum Inquiry* 47.1 (2017): 14–24.
10. As the UNHCR notes: "Only 61 per cent of refugee children attend primary school, compared with a global average of 92 per cent. As refugee children age, the obstacles to education increase. Just 23 per cent of refugee children are enrolled in secondary

school, compared to 84 per cent globally. For higher education the situation is critical. Only one per cent of refugees attend university, compared to 37 per cent globally." See https://www.unhcr.org/uk/education.html. [Accessed August 2019].
11 Sarah Dryden-Peterson (2017).
12 Silvia Pasquetti and Giovanni Picker, "Urban informality and confinement: toward a relational framework." *International Sociology* 32.4 (July 2017): 532–544.
13 Sylvia Chant with Craske Nikki, "Chapter 9 Gender and Migration" from Chant, Sylvia with, Craske, Nikki, *Gender in Latin America* (London: Latin American Bureau London, 2003), 228–253.
14 Doreen Indra, "Gender: A key dimension of the refugee experience." *Refuge: Canada's Journal on Refugees* (1987): 3–4.
15 Romola Sanyal, (2018).
16 Manas Ray, "Growing up refugee." *History Workshop Journal* 53.1. Oxford University Press (2002); Romola Sanyal, "Refugees and Urban poverty: a historical view from Calcutta." In Lemanski, C. and Marx, C. (eds.) *The City in Urban Poverty* (London: Palgrave Macmillan, 2015), 137–157.
17 Jennifer Hyndman and Wenona Giles, "Waiting for what? The feminization of asylum in protracted situations." *Gender, Place & Culture* 18.3 (2011): 361–379.
18 See Guy Standing, "Global feminization through flexible labor: A theme revisited." *World Development* 27.3 (1999): 583–602.
19 Doreen Indra, (1987).
20 Cathrine Brun, "Active Waiting and Changing Hopes." *Social Analysis* 59.1 (2015): 19–37.
21 Loren B. Landau, (2003).
22 Porter, Libby, Romola Sanyal, Synne Bergby, Kelly Yotebieng, Henrik Lebuhn, Magie M. Ramírez, Pedro Figueiredo Neto, and Simone Tulumello, "Borders and refuge: citizenship, mobility and planning in a volatile world/introduction: Urban planning and the global movement of people/planning for refugees in cities/the role of planning in humanitarian response, looking at Urban crisis response in Lebanon/Urban refugees: an Urban planning blind spot?/immigrant rights in Europe: planning the solidarity city/propertied liberalism in a Borderland city/displacement, refuge and Urbanisation: from refugee camps to ecovillages/from capitalist-Urbanisation ...." *Planning Theory & Practice* 20.1 (2019): 99–128.

PART IV

The contours of a long-term resolution

11
STATELESSNESS IN EXILE

Divita Shandilya

> The calamity of the rightless is not that they are deprived of life, liberty, and the pursuit of happiness, or of equality before the law and freedom of opinion but that they no longer belong to any community whatsoever. Their plight is not that they are not equal before the law, but that no law exists for them; not that they are oppressed but that nobody wants even to oppress them.
>
> Hannah Arendt – *On Origins of Totalitarianism*

Nationality determines the relationship between individual and the state. It enables a person to claim rights and protections in their country and under international law, thus according them the "right to have rights".[1] There are millions of people across the world, however, that live in a legal black hole because they have been denied nationality. They constitute the world's stateless population.

Stateless persons are often deprived of the most basic political and civil rights. They typically do not have identification documents due to which they are unable to go to schools or universities, get a job, get medical care, own property, or travel. They may not be able to legally register their marriages or the birth of their children. They may also be under threat of persecution and violence from members of religious or ethnic groups different from theirs, oftentimes with the sanction and even support of the state that is meant to protect them.

Contrast this with individuals who are recognized as nationals of a country and by implication have full political membership of its society. They are entitled to enjoy a gamut of political, social, economic, and cultural rights, including protection from discrimination and equality before the law. They have the right to reside in the territory of the country, the right to access basic services such as health and education, the right to own property and participate in economic activity, and the right to travel freely within the country and abroad among others. They are integrated into the international community by virtue of their nationality and have the right to protection provided by their country outside of its territory, including consular assistance and diplomatic protection.

The UNHCR estimates that there are at least 10 million stateless persons in the world.[2] The World's Stateless Report further says that there are around 3.5 million stateless refugees from Palestine and another at least 1.5 million stateless refugees, bringing the total tally to more than 15 million stateless persons worldwide.[3]

People may be reduced to a state of statelessness in the country that they would describe as their own – where they were born, have always lived, and have family ties.[4] The ruling dispensation may not recognize them as belonging to that country or it may rescind their existing status as nationals. A person can also be stateless in a migratory context, having lost nationality prior to or as a consequence of crossing an international border.[5]

But for stateless people who lack legal protection and rights due to the absence of a national identity, their vulnerabilities follow them everywhere. Their very existence is delegitimized, and they remain trapped in a cycle of poverty, abuse, and precarity, whether they are in the country whence they claim origin, or they are forced to leave. Rejected, rootless, and powerless, they are the wretched of the earth.

This chapter focuses on stateless persons who have been displaced. It begins by highlighting the myriad reasons which may render a person as a non-national and the impact it has on their ability to claim rights and protections in their country. It delves into the link between statelessness and displacement, as conditions which propagate statelessness may cause displacement, and sometimes displacement may lead to statelessness, especially in prolonged circumstances. It further examines the intergenerational nature of statelessness which puts the future of millions at risk and concludes with recommendations.

Making of statelessness

Some people are born stateless, others are made stateless. Statelessness can occur for several reasons, including gaps in nationality laws, the emergence of new states and transfer of territory between existing states, and discrimination in nationality laws which disenfranchise certain communities based on their ethnicity, gender, race, or religion.

Nationality laws that are written or applied too restrictively can cause statelessness at birth. For example, if a person's child is born in a foreign country which does not permit nationality based solely on birth in its territory, and if the country of origin does not allow any of the parents to pass on their nationality to their child, then this discrepancy may cause the child to be born without a nationality. Furthermore, countries with complex birth registration processes and weak administrative structures may inadvertently make it difficult for people to register their children at the time of birth.

Many countries have also retained gender discriminatory laws when it comes to citizenship. In certain countries, a woman may lose her nationality if she marries a man from another country. But she may not acquire the nationality of her husband, as the husband's country might require additional conditions to be fulfilled for the acquisition of nationality, such as a certain period of residence in the country.[6] There are also around 25 countries which do not allow women to pass on their nationality to their children. This puts children at imminent risk of statelessness in case their fathers are unknown, missing, or dead, especially in countries that do not adhere to nationality based on birth in their territory alone.

The formation of new states and restructuring of borders catalyses a process of nation-building which includes the state having to define who they consider to be nationals and who they exclude. This may result in the exclusion of entire communities whose religion, ethnicity, race, or language may be distinct from the majority community. Even when new countries allow nationality for all ethnic, racial, and religious minorities, specific groups or individuals may have trouble proving their links to the country and can be left without a nationality as a result.[7] The dissolution of states may also displace people from the territory they originally inhabited and leave them without the nationality of any country.

A case in point is that of the Sahrawi or Western Saharan people. When Spain withdrew from its colony of Western Sahara in 1976, no new state was established in its place and the people living there became stateless. Although the International Court of Justice ruled that the residents of the territory be allowed to vote in a referendum on the question of self-determination, Morocco soon assumed control of the territory, forcing thousands of people to flee into neighbouring Algeria. Currently, more than 90,000 Sahrawi live in refugee camps in Tindouf, Algeria, according to the UNHCR (though the Algerian government pegs this number at 165,000 people), and almost 26,000 Sahrawis live in Mauritania.[8]

The status of Western Sahara remains disputed to date and most of its people continue to live with an indeterminate nationality. Large swathes of Western Sahara are still controlled by Morocco, and the Moroccan government has recognised the residents as Moroccan nationals. But parts of it have been taken over by the Sahrawi liberation movement, the Polisario Front, which has declared these areas as the Sahrawi Arab Democratic Republic. This region is barely inhabited, however. At the same time, the Sahrawis who live in exile have neither been extended Algerian nationality nor do they qualify for nor desire Moroccan nationality. Instead, they proclaim the Sahrawi nationality, of a people without a land.

Individuals or communities who have neither received nationality automatically nor through government decision under the law of the land are known as de jure stateless persons.[9] There are also several others who do not have an effective nationality, that is they are unable to call upon their right to nationality for their protection, and are known as de facto stateless persons.[10] De facto stateless persons may be kept out of the ambit of formal citizenship by being refused a proof of nationality, residency, or other necessary documents which would establish their relationship with the state and allow them to access their rights.

The Rohingya people, who have been referred to as the most persecuted minority in the world, have experienced both de facto and de jure statelessness. Their citizenship rights, which were limited, to begin with, were revoked by the Myanmar Government in 1982.

Since the late 1970s, the Rohingya people have routinely faced harassment and oppression by the dominant Rakhine Buddhists and state authorities. They have also been victims of several spates of violence, including the outbreak in August 2017 which has been described as a textbook example of ethnic cleansing by the United Nations.[11] Thousands of Rohingya were killed, internally displaced, or fled into neighbouring Bangladesh to save their lives.

Noor, a young woman now living in Cox's Bazar's Ukhiya refugee camp, recalls the extortion and abuse that she and others of her community had to face in Myanmar.[12] Their lands and other property were forcefully seized and they were forced to work on the fields and in the homes of Rakhine Buddhists for meagre or no pay. They were frequently under threat of detention, torture, and sexual violence. Their movement was severely restricted, their children were unwelcomed in Burmese schools, and the Madrasas set up within the community were targeted by the armed forces. Hence kept from accessing education, healthcare, and livelihoods, the Rohingya largely lived in conditions of penury and emaciation.

Through it all, Rohingya people had no recourse against the violation of their rights. They could not turn to the authorities for help or organise amongst themselves as they were completely and systematically disempowered.

Samina, another Rohingya woman in the camp, wonders if her life would have been different had she been born anywhere but Myanmar. She is firm in her resolve to not go back to Rakhine unless the Myanmar Government recognises their Rohingya identity, accepts them as Myanmar nationals, and gives them equal rights as citizens of the country.

Stateless and displaced

The persistent persecution and marginalization of stateless persons can force them to leave the country they call home in search of safety and stability. It is estimated that one out of every three stateless persons in the world has been forcibly displaced, which is indicative of the strong connection between conditions of statelessness and displacement.[13] Though the immediate causes of displacement vary, the politics of deprivation and otherization of minority communities often results in the outbreak of violence which ends up pushing them out. In other cases, stateless persons may be physically removed from their home territory through forcible deportations or collective expulsions.[14] Stateless persons regularly find themselves in circumstances where they are vilified and under extreme distress with limited coping strategies, making fleeing the only viable option.

But their problems do not end there. Stateless persons who have been displaced are usually unable to access migratory routes through legal channels due to their lack of documents. They, therefore, have to go down the illicit route of forgers, traffickers, and smugglers, all of whom exploit them financially, mentally, and physically given their untenable situation.

They have little choice in picking their destination country, and once they reach the destination, they are completely at the discretion of the receiving government. Since stateless persons lack documentation and most countries do not have requisite procedures in place to identify and establish statelessness, host governments decide whether to treat them as refugees, who have the right to remain, or as migrants, who may not avail of the same protections. Worse, they may not be counted at all and remain as an undefined and unseen population on the margins, cut off from necessary aid and services.

Stateless persons are also vulnerable to being harassed and exploited in the host country as their presence in the country is illegal or disputed. They may be doubly persecuted as members of a minority and as an outsider in the host country, subjected to discriminatory laws, policies, and practices.[15] Their troubles are compounded as they have no legal or social standing in the adopted country and therefore cannot approach authorities or neighbours for help. There is both an enforced and a self-imposed process of invisibilisation – stateless persons prefer anonymity over intimidation by the state and its institutions.

Take the example of Mala, who escaped to India with her family from Sindh, Pakistan, when her son Raghu started receiving death threats following a dispute with local school authorities. Mala's husband was forced to approach agents to obtain visa documents when their official application was rejected. This costed them lakhs of rupees that they could ill-afford, but they were finally able to travel to India on religious visas. The touts who travelled with them had promised to take them to Jodhpur where Mala had relatives. But once they were across the border, they extracted more money from Mala's husband and forcibly sent them to Haridwar, threatening to expose them and get them jailed for violating their visa terms.

Mala and her family were left to fend for themselves and slowly made their way to Jodhpur. They were on the road for days, without any money and without shelter. They reached Jodhpur completely broke and without a place to stay. Their relatives were unable to support them because they too were living in miserable conditions. After a few weeks of being homeless, Mala and her husband managed to save enough money from daily wage labour to set up a shanty in the camp, where they stay in penury to this day.

Their children's education, which was the driving factor for the dispute and their eventual departure, was put on hold in India. Their sons could not get admitted to a school due to the lack of documents and ended up working with their parents as daily wage labourers to help with the finances.

People living in a state of statelessness are habitually under threat of being detained by authorities in the host country. For states that draw their authority from a social contract of fixed rights and obligations based on people's citizenship and "verifiable" roots in the territory, stateless persons are an inconvenience at best and a threat at worst. States uphold their end of the social contract through borders, documentation, orderliness, and increasing surveillance, and stateless persons, who by nature exist in an unstable social condition outside the nation state are considered to be a menace that needs to be controlled and contained.

The removal of stateless persons from society through long-term detention by host country authorities has emerged as a serious issue. Stateless people who are not recognized as refugees or are otherwise deemed not qualified to remain in the country lawfully, cannot be easily removed because they do not have a state of nationality to which they can be deported and their country of residence, from which they have fled or been expelled, may not take them back.[16] As removal from the territory becomes impossible, detention may become long term while governments attempt to figure out what to do with the people so detained. In countries with weak systems for processing asylum seekers and other forcibly displaced persons, stateless people face the prospect of being detained indefinitely, separated from families and forgotten by all else. This fear of detention may compel people to resort to progressively risky modes of survival and adopt negative coping mechanisms, thereby further endangering themselves.

Women and girls who are stateless face multiple barriers and challenges akin to other forcibly displaced women. But their vulnerability and deprivations are further intensified due to their lack of legal status in the host country. Their capacity to access aid and services such as education and healthcare might be inhibited; their exposure to gender-based violence and exploitation might be heightened; and their ability to work might be severely curtailed, forcing them to seek sustenance through perilous means. These impacts may be felt even more acutely by single women, who have lost or have been separated from their family members and other community members. Not only do they lack identity as a legal entity which would enable them to approach the government or NGOs, but they are also devoid of the social safety net provided by family and friends, which is often all that stateless persons have.

Statelessness in abeyance

Stateless persons are at high risk of passing on their statelessness to their children. Their country's government may not allow them to register the birth of their children or it may summarily refuse to recognize their children's nationality.

In situations of forced displacement, birth registration can be equally challenging as the host country may actively adopt a policy discouraging the registration of children born to foreigners or refugees, even singling out a particular refugee community in some instances.[17] Additionally, displaced persons may lack awareness of the procedure to register births or may not have access to authorities responsible for birth registration due to restrictions on freedom of movement or encampment. They may also not be able to afford a costly or lengthy registration process. Stateless persons can be further disadvantaged in this regard as they may lack the necessary documents to prove their nationality and their so-called legal non-existence might propel the host country government to refrain from registering their children.

Thus, being already deprived of citizenship in their home countries and denied legal recognition in the host country, children of stateless persons are condemned to growing up without a nationality, carrying on the inter-generational condition of their family or community. It is also highly likely that children who arrive in the host country as unaccompanied minors or orphans may never get the chance to be registered as refugees or to establish their nationality.

For women, who normally flee conflict areas alone as their husbands might be part of the fighting factions or maybe missing or dead, this risk of not being able to pass on their nationality is even more acute. Some of these women are pregnant at the time of displacement, and others might have conceived as a result of rape before or during their journey of escape. When they give birth in the host country, the newborn might not be registered there, putting them at the risk of statelessness, especially if they cannot inherit their mother's nationality. For example, Syrian nationality law does not allow women to transfer their nationality to their children, so the babies of Syrian refugee women could potentially be stateless if their mothers are unable to prove their descent from a Syrian father.[18]

Statelessness can also be created in cases of protracted displacements. After being forced to spend generations abroad, a displaced community's ties with the country of origin may be lost and it could cease to consider them as nationals, while access to nationality of the host country may remain out of their reach.[19]

As statelessness is passed from one generation to another, the cycle of poverty, abuse, and precarity is reinforced. The children of stateless persons live an extremely uncertain life with little or no access to education, healthcare, or other essential services, and then grow up with few livelihood avenues, limited freedoms, and virtually no rights and protection.

It is rare for stateless people to achieve integration, relocation, or repatriation – the so-called durable solutions which typify refugee movements. The hurdles in integrating with local populations in host countries have already been illustrated above. It is also highly improbable for them to be able to relocate to another country from the host country because of the lack of recognition and documentation, unless they are from communities which are under the mandate of international organisations such as UNHCR and the United Nations Relief and Works Agency for Palestine Refugees (UNWRA) who may be able to support them in relocation.

Stateless persons also find it harder to return to their country of origin, as the country of origin may continue to uphold their statelessness and deny them entry. They may also be unable to repatriate if the country of origin has ceased to exist as a state in the aftermath of a civil war or is yet to be recognized as an independent state, as in the case of Western Sahara. So, they are left in a predicament: remain in the country of asylum and hope for integration, or return, but with little guarantee of any meaningful change to the status quo.[20]

Bintou, a Sahrawi woman was born in a refugee camp in Tindouf, Algeria, in 1986. She is now the mother of two young children. She grew up on stories of the war, of how families were torn apart, and of how her parents were forced to watch their parents die in front of their eyes. She says that there will be no relief or resolution for the Sahrawi people unless they live in an independent country of their own. Until then, their lives are a long-drawn-out period of waiting and coping and hoping for something better.

The lack of options for stateless populations adds to their loss of agency and insecurity. They are forced to spend their lives struggling to assert and legitimize their being.

Conclusion

This chapter attempts to capture the multiple vulnerabilities of people who are without a nationality and have been forcibly displaced. They are marginalised and targeted in their countries and are accorded little to no protection if they leave.

Being stateless can have a profound psychological impact on people as they lose their sense of belongingness and community and may feel rejected and forgotten. Over time they are left with little hope of improvement in their conditions, even as they are helpless in preventing their statelessness from being passed down to their children.

Statelessness is an ascendant phenomenon. The number of cases of children who were born into statelessness was higher than the number of cases of statelessness that were resolved in both 2016 and 2017.[21] The causes of statelessness lay bare the fundamental conflict at the heart of the perpetuation of this phenomenon – the conflict between state sovereignty and its role as the principal guarantor of human rights and the universality of human rights enshrined in international law.

The international human rights framework asserts that every individual has a right to nationality, yet governments ultimately decide who they deem to be nationals of the country. Considerations of race and ethnicity frequently play a major role in the design and application of nationality laws. This is manifested in the privileging of the principle of blood origin (jus sanguinis) over birth on the territory (jus soli) in recognizing people as nationals. It can make the inclusion of minorities difficult, particularly of relatively recent migrants and children of migrants.[22]

It can also intensify the process of exclusion. While cases of statelessness may well be attributed to legal lacunae and technicalities at times, it is apparent that the leading cause is arbitrary deprivation of nationality, including on the basis of racial, ethno-religious, and gender discrimination.[23] And given the centrality of nationality to the assertion of state sovereignty, it is to be expected that international laws and norms can only go so far in ensuring that people are not stripped of their nationality by state action. In the event of such state action, the remedial and punitive options available under international law are severely limited, especially if stateless persons continue to stay in the country where they are under attack.

But when stateless persons are displaced, it must serve both as a call to action and as an opportunity for the international community. Host country governments, multilateral organisations, and humanitarian organisations should set up systems to identify and establish statelessness and ensure that stateless persons are not ignored or criminalized in the event of displacement.[24] At the outset, they must provide them with access to first aid, food rations, healthcare and counselling, critical information, and water and sanitation. They must set up mechanisms to assess the differential needs of women and children and other vulnerable groups and respond accordingly.

The host country governments should also provide stateless persons with basic identification and documentation, including to their newborn children. This would allow them to avoid harassment from local authorities, protect them from arbitrary detention in the host country, and enable them to enroll their children in schools or in non-formal education programmes and access jobs in the informal economy. They should encourage and facilitate stateless people in approaching the legal system in the host country to protect themselves from exploitation and violence.

As detailed earlier, stateless persons are often unable to leave the territory where they are being persecuted to access safety and when they do so, they can be denied recognition as refugees due to their lack of nationality and requisite documents. For instance, many Rohingya people who have fled from Myanmar to neighbouring countries are not recognized as refugees. Both the governments of Thailand and India have chosen to term the Rohingya in their territory as illegal immigrants in recent times, and even the Bangladesh government refers to the Rohingya who have arrived since 2017 as forcibly displaced Myanmar nationals.[25]

These designations invariably have deep implications for the obligations placed on host country governments, the remit and approach of international agencies, and the range of protections and rights available to the displaced populations. In response, the UNHCR should work along with governments to devise and negotiate internationally recognized travel documents for stateless persons similar to the Nansen passport which would first allow them to access safe migration routes and leave their country and secondly, apply for asylum in other countries.[26]

The 1954 Convention relating to the Status of Stateless persons sets out the rights to which stateless persons are entitled and mirrors the 1951 Refugee Convention.[27] However, there are significant differences which make it less comprehensive, most notably the lack of protection against refoulement and against penalization for illegal entry.[28] Furthermore, the overarching principle of the 1954 Convention as regards treatment is that contracting states shall accord to stateless persons the same treatment as is accorded to aliens in general.[29] This may undermine the special protection needs of stateless people and keep them from receiving vital welfare.

Therefore, it is imperative for states to extend similar protections to displaced stateless persons as they do to refugees. Since stateless persons are fleeing from persecution, torture, or discrimination that international refugee law is designed to protect forcibly displaced persons from, states must also fulfil their obligation of non-refoulement to them.

In addition, any attempt at relocation or repatriation must be subject to the conditions laid down for the repatriation of refugees and must be safe, dignified, and voluntary. It must be based on ensuring that the nationality of stateless persons is recognized by the country of origin or the country to which they are relocating and that they are provided full citizenship rights.

Statelessness invariably begets an irreversible dehumanization.[30] These steps are but a small beginning in attempting to humanize the lived conditions of stateless persons and enabling them to rebuild and lead dignified lives.

Notes

1 Arendt, Hannah, 1906–1975, 1973, *The origins of totalitarianism*. New York, Harcourt Brace Jovanovich.
2 Van Waas, Laura, Chickera, Amal De and Albarazi, Zahra, December 2014, The world's stateless: a new report on why size does and doesn't matter, *European Network on Statelessness*.
3 Institute on Statelessness and Inclusion, December 2014, *The world's stateless*, Wolf Legal Publishers, available at http://www.institutesi.org/worldsstateless.pdf. Accessed on June 10, 2019.
4 Institute on Statelessness and Inclusion, December 2014, *The world's stateless*, Wolf Legal Publishers, available at http://www.institutesi.org/worldsstateless.pdf. Accessed on June 10, 2019.
5 Institute on Statelessness and Inclusion, December 2014, *The world's stateless*, Wolf Legal Publishers, available at http://www.institutesi.org/worldsstateless.pdf. Accessed on June 10, 2019.
6 Edwards, Alice and Van Waas, Laura, 2014, *The Oxford Handbook of refugee and forced migration studies*, Oxford: Oxford University Press.
7 UNHCR, *Ending statelessness*, available at https://www.unhcr.org/stateless-people.html. Accessed on June 9, 2019.
8 Institute on Statelessness and Inclusion, December 2014, *The world's stateless*, Wolf Legal Publishers, available at http://www.institutesi.org/worldsstateless.pdf. Accessed on June 10, 2019.
9 Blitz, Brad K., 2009, Stateless, protection, equality, *Forced Migration Policy Briefing 3*, Refugee Studies Centre.
10 Blitz, Brad K., 2009, Stateless, protection, equality, *Forced Migration Policy Briefing 3*, Refugee Studies Centre.
11 Human Rights Council 36th session, Opening Statement by Zeid Ra'ad Al Hussein, United Nations High Commissioner for Human Rights, September 2017, available at https://www.ohchr.org/EN/NewsEvents/Pages/DisplayNews.aspx?NewsID=22041&LangID=E. Accessed on 11 June 2019.
12 The examples referred to in the chapter are from the narratives presented in Chapter 3 of this volume, unless specified otherwise.
13 Albarazi, Zahra and Van Waas, Laura, Stateless and Displacement: Scoping Paper, Tilburg University, 2016.

14 Albarazi, Zahra and Van Waas, Laura, Stateless and Displacement: Scoping Paper, Tilburg University, 2016.
15 Chickera, Amal De and Whiteman, Joanna, May 2014, Discrimination and the human security of stateless people, *Forced Migration Review* 46.
16 Perks, Katherine and Clifford, Jarlath, April 2009, The legal limbo of detention, *Forced Migration Review* 32.
17 Albarazi, Zahra and Van Waas, Laura, Stateless and Displacement: Scoping Paper, Tilburg University, 2016.
18 Albarazi, Zahra and Van Waas, Laura, 2016, Understanding Statelessness in the Syrian Context, Institute on Stateless and Inclusion.
19 Albarazi, Zahra and Van Waas, Laura, Stateless and Displacement: Scoping Paper, Tilburg University, 2016.
20 Faulkner, C. and Schiffer, S., 2019, *Unwelcomed? The effects of statelessness on involuntary refugee repatriation in Bangladesh and Myanmar.* The Round Table, 1–14.
21 Institute on Statelessness and Inclusion, 2018, Statelessness in numbers: An overview and analysis of global statistics. The UNHCR has estimated that in the five largest non-refugee statelessness situations alone, 70,000 children are born into statelessness each year.
22 Blitz, Brad K., 2009, Stateless, protection, equality, *Forced Migration Policy Briefing 3*, Refugee Studies Centre.
23 Foster, Michelle and Lambert, Helene, 2016, Statelessness as a Human Rights Issue: A concept whose time has come, *International Journal of Refugee Law*, 28(4), 564–584.
24 Any such identification system must encompass people who are de facto stateless and do not fit refugee criteria, but are at risk of persecution, discrimination, or de jure statelessness and hence cannot return home.
25 Rohingyas are forcibly displaced Myanmar nationals, not refugees, *The Daily Star*, September 28, 2017, available at https://www.thedailystar.net/world/rohingya-c risis/rohingyas-are-forcibly-displaced-myanmar-nationals-not-refugees-1468999. Accessed on June 11, 2019.
26 In 1922, the first head of the Office of the High Commissioner for Refugees, Fridtjof Nansen, introduced and obtained states' agreement to a "Nansen certificate" which was the first legal instrument used for the international protection of refugees, available at https://www.unhcr.org/events/nansen/4aae50086/nansen-man-action-vision.html. Accessed on June 11, 2019.
27 *The Equal Rights Trust, Unravelling Anomaly Detention, Discrimination and the Protection Needs of Stateless Persons*, 2010.
28 *The Equal Rights Trust, Unravelling Anomaly Detention, Discrimination and the Protection Needs of Stateless Persons*, 2010.
29 Statelessness, Alice Edwards and Laura Van Waas, *The Oxford Handbook of Refugee and Forced Migration Studies*, 2014.
30 Bhargava, Rajeev, The state of statelessness, *The Hindu*, August 2018, available at https://www.thehindu.com/opinion/columns/the-state-of-statelessness/article 24604306.ece. Accessed on June 12, 2019.

12
REFUGEE REPATRIATION

The role of education, healthcare, livelihood, and violence

Mollie Gerver

The media often describes refugees returning home because war has ended.[1] In reality, refugees often choose to repatriate or remain abroad for a multitude of reasons, some only indirectly related to war.

Between 2012 and 2018, I attempted to better understand the different circumstances and experiences of refugees who repatriated or remained abroad, interviewing 33 women and 10 girls who had recently returned from Israel to South Sudan, or who had again left South Sudan for Uganda. I interviewed an additional nine South Sudanese women in Nairobi who had never left East Africa, but who had similarly returned to South Sudan or who had chosen to refrain from repatriating. These interviews were part of a broader project that included 193 interviews with refugees who had repatriated to various countries around the globe, including Sudan, Eritrea, Thailand, and the Philippines.

When I asked the women what their reasons were for repatriating, nearly all gave answers that were not directly related to war, but their lack of access to four central rights in host countries: the right to education, the right to basic livelihoods, the right to healthcare, and the right to freedom from violence. Of those who decided not to repatriate, or who chose to leave South Sudan after repatriating, most cited this same lack of rights as their reason for remaining abroad.

The role of education

The first woman I spoke to, who described education as a central reason for repatriating, was Ajouk.

At the age of four Ajouk fled with her parents from Aweil, South Sudan, to Khartoum. She married at the age of 16, never obtaining a formal education. Years later, she crossed from Egypt into Israel, began working, but never went

DOI: 10.4324/9781003047094-12

to school. In 2011, she decided that this needed to change. The only way she felt she could obtain an education was to return to Aweil, a town she knew almost nothing about, but which she knew had adult education classes. When I spoke with her in 2012, she had yet to sign up for classes, spending most of her time caring for her younger siblings. But she had plans to enrol and hoped this would become a reality once her siblings had completed secondary school.[2]

The case of Ajouk was somewhat unique; most individuals I spoke with did not return to access adult education for themselves, but education for their children. Like the majority of refugee children around the world,[3] many refugee children in Israel could not access the public education system in 2010. This was the year mothers began returning to Aweil with their children, often as their husbands remained in Israel. Once in Aweil, they had to start bearing the costs of education, but managed to put aside enough to send their children to school.

I asked 15-year-old Ayen how school was now that she was in her country of citizenship.

She spoke about books and basketball: she missed both. While in Israel she had access to a library and could play basketball, steadily improving over the course of her childhood. She thought about playing football in Aweil but was told that only boys play sports.

This slowly transformed during Ayen's first year in South Sudan. While walking around her neighbourhood in 2012, we stopped at a large plot of land with two goal posts and two football teams comprised of secondary school girls. The girls were dressed in shorts and t-shirts, rare for the neighbourhood, where women and girls were largely dressed in traditional Dinka clothes, and where policemen would sometimes stop girls wearing trousers, ordering them to put on a skirt. The football players were passing the football back and forth, often running from a coach who had a whip, which he cracked when a girl was too slow. This was a common mechanism for encouraging faster speed and agility on the field. "At least he trains the girls like the boys," one of Ayen's friends wryly noted. It was a new football programme, organised by returnees who had lived in Kenya, Uganda, and other countries in East Africa. As we sat on the side and watched the game with other onlookers, Ayen considered joining. She ultimately decided against it, afraid of the whip.[4]

Girls' education was not only a reason why some returned to South Sudan. It was also a reason why many left. I interviewed 14 girls in Uganda, along with 8 of their mothers. The 14 girls had returned to South Sudan essentially because they did not wish to live in detention in Israel, a new requirement from 2012. Once in South Sudan they learned that education was difficult to access. For some, this was because they were expected, by their extended family members, to spend their time doing household chores. For most, their parents simply could not afford to pay the school fees. The girls' challenges were not unique for South Sudan: two-thirds of girls in the country do not attend school, the highest rate in the world.[5] Fortunately, within a year their friends in Israel had raised money for their education in Uganda.

One girl from South Sudan who made this move to Uganda was Nyadhial. She was 16 when she returned from Israel to South Sudan with her parents, eventually living in a village in the north of the country. Her parents lacked money for school fees, and so she had to stay at home even as the other children went to school. This changed two months later, when she received a phone call from friends in Israel who had raised money for her education in Entebbe. Much relieved, today she studies in a boarding school.

Though she is happy to be in school, when I interviewed her in 2013, she complained of racism by some teachers:

> If one South Sudanese does something, they will say "the Sudanese do this", not the name of the one Sudanese student who did it. Like if I were to do something wrong, they would not say "Nyadhial did it", but "the Sudanese did this". For example, once there was this girl who got into a fight with a Ugandan girl and hit her. Rather than upbraiding the girl, the teachers talked about all the Sudanese doing something wrong.

Conditions have substantially improved in the school since I last spoke with Nyadhial but, even if they hadn't, she says she would have still remained in Uganda. The benefits of obtaining an education are more important for her than the benefits of avoiding racism.[6]

The girls in Uganda who returned from Israel to South Sudan were relatively privileged: they had friends in Israel who helped them in their quest for education. Less privileged refugees I spoke with similarly described education as a key reason for leaving South Sudan again after repatriating and choosing to not repatriate in the near future. For example, Nyabol and her husband had left South Sudan on numerous occasions throughout their lives, eventually arriving in Israel in 2006, and returning to South Sudan with their four children in 2012. When they arrived, they lacked access to clean water, food, and education, and so in September 2013, they travelled with their children to Kakuma refugee camp in Kenya, where their children received these necessities. Shortly after, they returned to South Sudan to seek legal work and send money to their children who remained in Kakuma. They failed to find work, and when war broke out, they went to the IDP camp in Juba. Both lack the money to travel to Kenya to be with their children, but do not wish their children to repatriate. While their children might access security and food in the IDP camp in Juba, they would not have access to reliable schooling.[7]

South Sudanese women and girls in Nairobi, who had spent their entire lives in East Africa, similarly chose to remain in Kenya for education rather than repatriate. However, unlike the women and girls who had returned from Israel, actually accessing education was a greater challenge for them. Consider the case of Mary, born in 1988 in Akobo, South Sudan. Mary was a young toddler when her mother became infected during childbirth, and so together they left South Sudan for medical treatment in Itang in Ethiopia. Once there her mother did get treatment, but when fighting broke out, they decided to move to Kenya, arriving at Kakuma refugee camp in 1993. One reason for remaining in Kakuma was that Mary could attend school, but Mary's plans were dashed when she was forced to marry at the age of 14. Her husband forbade her from attending school, and she has had no formal education since.[8]

The role of livelihoods

Though Mary never continued her formal education, she learned technically sophisticated beadwork methods from other women in Kakuma, enabling her to create impressive square tapestries. And while many women have beadwork skills, the quality of Mary's work stands out. She selects colours, shapes, and clever interconnected patterns that would likely sell well in an upscale gallery.

She lacks an upscale gallery, and so throughout the 2000s, she made a small income selling beadwork to other camp residents and selling food from a small kitchen she had established. "The bachelors in Kakuma cannot cook," she said, "and so I sold food to them". She remained in the camp despite additional challenges arising in 2010. That year her husband died, and her three children were taken away from her by his family and brought to Gambella in Ethiopia. She wanted to follow her children and try to get them back, but her late husband's family threatened to harm her if she tried to do so.

After a year, she began a relationship with a man and together they had a child, but he was physically abusive. When she attempted to go to the police, her partner would pay them a bribe to avoid arrest. She even approached a UN protection officer but was told that only the police could rein him in, as only they could investigate crimes. Frustrated, she used the remaining money she had to travel to Nairobi, where she stayed with friends in a room in the suburbs of Ruiru. Together they created beadwork but lacked a reliable market.

This seemed to change in 2016, when Mary was approached by a woman from the United States who agreed to try and sell her pieces there and send money if any were sold. Mary gave her the beadwork she had completed, but she never heard back from her again, losing hundreds of dollars in assets. Frustrated, she decided to take a pause in her life, rest for a month, and think about how to proceed. By the end of the month she decided to pour her remaining money, roughly 300 USD, into a tailoring course. This was risky as she did not have a work permit, like the vast majority of South Sudanese living in Kenya. She was unlikely to get employment even if she gained tailoring skills. But she was anxious to do something, and against all odds did obtain temporary employment at a bag-making factory a month after completing her course. Today she no longer has employment but is confident that making money in Kenya without a work visa is easier than doing so in South Sudan with citizenship. For this reason, she has no intention of returning "home", a country she has not lived in since leaving it with her mother in the early 1990s.[9]

There were other women who, like Mary, decided to remain abroad to support themselves with small businesses. One such woman was Tareza, who at the start of the interview described to me her life in her home village in South Sudan, where at the age of 15 she grew close to a young man. She smiles as she recalls their earlier courtship, which led to marriage soon after. She laughs when I ask her if she married voluntarily. "Yes! I was in love!" After marriage they travelled to Juba where he found a job and she opened a small business. Every day she would embroider bedsheets using traditional South Sudanese methods, stitching colourful threads into uber-realistic flowers, animals, and trees. She would sell each one for over a hundred dollars, making a decent income along with her husband. Still, their money felt increasingly insufficient as prices rose dramatically throughout Juba. In 2009, they decided she would move to Dadaab in Kenya with their children, as the South Sudanese currency was especially strong, and she could continue to sell embroidery in the camp, obtaining free food and schooling for their children. He would remain behind in Juba, sending her remittances.

Tareza and her husband's decision made strategic sense. The diversity of their income sources – her small business, her husband's job in Juba and the UN's aid programme – meant that even if one of their sources dried up, another would likely remain. But in 2013 their plans fell apart. That year civil war broke out in Juba, and her husband was killed. Two years later she managed to save enough money to travel to Juba and confirm her husband's death, while her children remained behind in Dadaab to access food and education. She did not intend to return to South Sudan permanently: not only was it unsafe, but the insecurity meant there were fewer markets for her embroidery. Without embroidery sales, she would lack money to pay for shelter and food for her children, let alone school fees. For two years she lived in an IDP camp in Juba, and finally collected enough money to return to her children in Kenya in 2018. Today she sells embroidered sheets in Dadaab and has no plans of repatriating in the near future. While she feels that her rights in Kenya are limited, given that she cannot legally access formal markets, the informal business that she has maintained is crucial for her survival.[10]

The role of healthcare

Many individuals I spoke with suffered from health-related complications upon repatriating. Of the 48 children whose medical conditions I could confirm post-repatriation from Israel, 3 died of malaria within the first two years, representing over 6 per cent of my sample.[11] It is no wonder that the parents felt the pressure to leave. For example, one couple was initially repatriated from Israel to South Sudan in 2012 with their children, and soon after, their first child died of malaria. When their second child also contracted malaria, they took a bus to a very insecure area with a Medicines Sans Frontier clinic, received treatment and immediately contacted family friends in Canada to help them obtain resettlement. They succeeded and have no plans to repatriate today.[12]

In Nairobi, three women chose to leave Kakuma and Dadaab refugee camps and arrived in Nairobi to obtain medical treatment. They similarly have no plans to repatriate because of the poor medical care infrastructure in South Sudan. For example, Elisabeth was living in Kakuma when her daughter began having severe chest pain accompanied by difficulty in breathing. She took her to a doctor in Kakuma, but he could not diagnose the problem, and the medicine she received was ineffective. Elisabeth decided that Nairobi was the best option for medical care, and they travelled there, attempting to raise funds from friends and family to pay for an examination at a hospital. She had yet to find enough donations by the end of 2018 but has no plans to repatriate: despite her frustrations with the medical care in Kakuma, she feels it is better than what she would receive in South Sudan.

The role of domestic violence and conflict

While most women I spoke with decided where to live based on food, shelter, health, and education, a small number decided where to live based on access to security from abuse. One such woman was Adut who, in 2010, faced physical violence from her father while in Israel. She complained to a social worker, who recommended that she live in a boarding school meant especially for children facing domestic violence. At first, this seemed like a good idea, but she was afraid that if her parents were deported from Israel, she might be separated from her mother permanently. In 2012, when her parents were threatened with imprisonment if they remained in Israel, she decided to repatriate to South Sudan with them. Shortly after repatriating, Adut went to study in a boarding school in Kenya. While one reason for remaining in Kenya was to continue her education, an important second reason was to avoid abuse at home.[13]

For three women, the threat of abuse impacted their reasons not for leaving South Sudan, but for initially repatriating. Nyandeng originally fled South Sudan for Egypt as a young girl, and as an adult crossed over into Israel with her husband and their four children. While in Israel she faced abuse by her husband while pregnant with their fifth child. She separated from him as a result. She later suffered from post-partum psychosis, attempting to kill their son the moment he was born. As a result, her son was taken from her and placed in foster care, while she fell into a deep depression. When her husband repatriated with their four older children without her consent, she chose to repatriate to re-obtain the custody of her children. In 2011, she succeeded in re-obtaining the custody of only one of her children.

Soon after interviewing Nyandeng, I received a phone call from a reporter in Israel. Nyandeng's mother had managed to obtain resettlement in Australia and was coming to Israel to obtain custody of her grandson, Nyandeng's son, Avram. She succeeded, and Avram now lives in Australia. I tried to call Nyandeng in South Sudan and ask her if it was possible for her to obtain a visa to live in Australia with her mother and son. I was unsuccessful in contacting her for years, and so were her mother and the reporter. As of 2015, Nyandeng remained missing.[14]

While Nyandeng and Adut faced abuse by immediate family members, some faced abuse by extended family members. Sarah married as a second wife when she was 15, and her husband's first wife committed suicide soon after. The first wife's family blamed Sarah for the suicide and threatened to harm her. So, Sarah and her husband left South Sudan for a refugee camp in Kenya. Years later, she came face to face with the first wife's family when they moved into the same camp. She describes their meeting:

> I met them and we fought in the market while I was pregnant. This was March 2014. When they saw me, they said, "you think you escaped from us because your husband brought you here." They punched me even though I was pregnant, and I had to undergo an operation because of the punching. The baby was not even breathing inside so they had to operate so it would not die.

Sarah's reasons for leaving South Sudan, and not returning, were partly to avoid abuse from the first wife's family, and this reason was clearly not relevant once the family arrived in the same camp. But today she has new reasons for not returning – she relies on UN medical care and food rations to survive.[15]

Complex cases

The above cases are organised into simplified categorisations. I described women suffering on account of lack of education, livelihoods, health, or security. But many of these women experienced two or more of these factors: Sarah experienced both abuse and lack of healthcare and food in South Sudan. Adut experienced both abuse and lack of education in South Sudan. These and other women demonstrate how complex decision-making can be.

This complexity is especially clear from a final case, that of Martha.

Martha grew up in Bentiu, South Sudan. She married at the age of 17 and travelled with her husband to Kenya, partly because of the outbreak of violence, but largely because she and her husband wished to ensure that they could obtain a formal education for their future children. Her husband eventually repatriated to South Sudan in 2010 to work as a mechanic and would send money to her and their four children in Nairobi. In 2013, with the outbreak of the South Sudanese civil war, her husband went missing.

One result of her husband going missing was her inability to pay rent for her small home in Ruiru, a suburb of Nairobi. She was told by her landlord that she must leave the rental house and remain in a small corrugated metal shack next to the property until she could pay the overdue rent. If she moved out of the shack without paying the rent, he would call the police and have her arrested. As a result, she felt she could not move to Dadaab or Kakuma refugee camps or return to South Sudan: if she tried either, she would be stopped by the police and imprisoned for failing to pay overdue rent.

Though Martha did not want to remain in the small metal shack, she was also grateful that she had at least some shelter. She told me that the landlord's threat was a mix of financial interest and sympathy: he wanted the overdue rent amount, but he did not force her to live on the street, and she was free to walk around, visit friends, seek employment and send her children to school if she managed to find money for fees. The shack, she says, was better than what she would have in South Sudan, even if potentially worse than what she might obtain in Dadaab and Kakuma, where homes were sometimes available with better protection against the rain. Her reasons for not repatriating, she said, were therefore a combination of fear of arrest and the ability to have some type of shelter in Nairobi.[16]

Conclusion

The cases of Martha, and the other women I spoke to, paint a nuanced picture of repatriation – individuals do not leave their country only because of war, or return only when war is over. They leave and return for a multitude of interconnected factors, including education, livelihoods, health and domestic security. And these factors need not follow a simple narrative. Violence and lack of necessities take many forms and understanding these forms can clarify why women make the choices they do, and why their choices are constrained.

The women mentioned here raise a broader issue: displacement is not a single event that ends with return. It is an event that can occur multiple times, with each displacement raising new challenges abroad, and each repatriation entailing new risks at home.

For repatriation to be a truly durable solution – for women to feel that they can return without constantly worrying if they must leave again – they must be able to assert their rights to development. Such development should include both formal procedures as well as special resources when the formal procedures fail. Women must be able to access security against violence when the police do not help. They must be able to access healthcare that is free when money is lacking. They must be able to access food that is adequate for health, and not only limited rations in a far-away camp. And they must have a say in how security, healthcare, food, and schooling are provided. Doing so will not only increase their agency, but it will also improve their ability to plan their lives, empowering them to return when they are ready, and accessing rights when they are not.

Notes

1 When I Google-searched "refugees returning home" and "refugees repatriating," the top search results described refugees not returning to Syria because the war continues, and refugees not returning to Myanmar because of continued persecution.
2 Interview with Ajouk, Aweil, March 26, 2013.
3 Sonia Elks, "Less than Half of the World's Refugee Children are Enrolled in School," *World Economic Forum*, August 31, 2018, accessed on April 30, 2019 from https://ww

w.weforum.org/agenda/2018/08/less-than-half-of-refugee-children-enrolled-in-school-u-n.
4 Interview with Ayen, Aweil, March 25, 2012.
5 The rates may be higher in Somalia and Syria, but there is insufficient data in these countries. See Adela Suliman, "Going to School? Unlikely if You're a Girl in South Sudan, Report Says," Reuters, October 10, 2017, accessed on April 30, 2019, from https://www.reuters.com/article/us-women-education/going-to-school-unlikely-if-youre-a-girl-in-south-sudan-report-says-idUSKBN1CF01S.
6 Interview with Nyadhial, Entebbe, May 13, 2013.
7 Interview with Nyabol, Tong Ping IDP camp, Juba, January 2, 2014.
8 Interview with Mary, Ruriu, February 10, 2016.
9 Interview with Mary, Ruriu, February 10, 2016.
10 Interview with Tareza, Ruriu, February 11, 2018.
11 Mollie Gerver, *The Ethics and Practice of Refugee Repatriation*, Edinbirgh: Ediburgh University Press, 2018.
12 Interview with Gatwetch, Addis Ababa, June 12, 2014.
13 Interviews with Adut, Nairobi, May 4, 5, and 7, 2013.
14 Interview with Nyandeng, Aweil, March 30, 2012.
15 Interview with Sarah, Ruiru, February 10, 2018.
16 Interview with Martha, Nairobi, February 9, 2018.

13

TOWARDS DURABLE SOLUTIONS

The rights of refugees and shared responsibilities of states to ensure their protection

Rebecca Dowd

Introduction

It is a distressingly well-known fact that global displacement figures are at an all-time high, with the record again being broken in 2017.[1] There is no sign of this relenting in the near future. Yet commitment by states to providing protection, assistance, and durable solutions in a spirit of international solidarity appears to be waning.[2]

The main threat to the international protection regime is not – as some would claim – that the international legal framework is out of date. The framework is sound and is supplemented as required by normative and soft law at the national, regional, and international levels, to ensure that it can respond to emerging needs. The recently adopted, non-binding Global Compact on Refugees,[3] for example, has strengthened the international protection regime by helping to fill one of its most critical, persistent gaps: the lack of guidance on how states should share the responsibility for large-scale displacement crises.

The main threat to the international protection regime stems from its inconsistent and unpredictable implementation by states. By exploring the experiences of women and girls throughout their tumultuous displacement journeys, this book sheds light on the devastating impact that lack of adequate protection and assistance in line with international norms can have on the lives of women and girls.

Unequal access to resources and limited education and employment opportunities, for example, can economically disempower women, leaving them destitute and driving some to resort to risky coping strategies. As mentioned throughout this book, insufficient prevention of and protection against sexual and gender-based violence can expose women and girls to abuse and harm, hampering their ability to thrive. National legislation that perpetuates gender inequality can

DOI: 10.4324/9781003047094-13

further embed cultural perceptions of women as inferior and inherently weak, leading to reduced opportunities for social and economic participation, disregard for women's skills and potential, and, as a result, low levels of self-esteem and self-respect among women themselves.

The international refugee law framework

The international legal framework – with the 1951 Convention on the Status of Refugees and its 1967 Protocol at its core – is strong. Everyone has the right to seek asylum[4] and states are prohibited from returning a person to a country where his or her life and safety would be at risk.[5] International human rights law sets standards for the treatment of all people, while international refugee law sets minimum standards for the treatment of refugees, including with respect to accessing courts, primary education, work, and certain documentation.[6]

The international refugee law framework has been supplemented by several regional refugee and subsidiary protection instruments over the years,[7] and continues to grow in light of developments in international human rights law. Soft law instruments such as declarations, General Assembly resolutions and UNHCR Executive Committee Conclusions indicate states' ongoing commitment to, as well as their evolving understanding of, their obligations under international refugee law.

Yet there are notable gaps in the international refugee protection regime. Most obviously, the international legal framework only applies to those states that have acceded to the relevant instruments. Even then, some states have lodged reservations, thereby restricting their obligations.

Further, the protections set out in international refugee law only apply to people who are deemed to fit the legal definition of a refugee. Consider, for example, people who are forcibly displaced across an international border for non-refugee-related reasons such as natural disasters, climate change or severe socio-economic deprivation. Or those whose need for (non-persecution-related) protection arises when they are already outside their country of origin, such as stranded migrants or displaced migrant workers.[8] Such people will not, in most circumstances, meet the definition of a refugee as prescribed in the 1951 Convention, though they may have a legitimate need for protection.

National, regional, and international laws and instruments have gone some way to addressing gaps such as these,[9] but there is no comprehensive framework in place for the protection of people in "refugee-like" situations. It is noteworthy that the Programme of Action, which forms part of the recently adopted Global Compact on Refugees, recognises that "external forced displacement may result from sudden-onset natural disasters and environmental degradation."[10]

Inconsistencies in the interpretation of the refugee definition between states further complicates the picture, giving rise to the unfortunate reality that a person may be accepted as a refugee in one country but refused in another.

Gaps in the 1951 Convention extend beyond the refugee definition. For example, the 1951 Convention does not set standards for admission to territory, access to asylum procedures, the protection of asylum-seekers, responses to protracted situations or large-scale influxes, protection at sea, secondary movements or the timely pursuit of durable solutions. Over time, a number of these gaps have been addressed in Executive Committee conclusions, General Assembly resolutions, and inter-state agreements, but some still remain.[11]

A significant gap in the international refugee protection regime – which has emerged since the inception of the 1951 Convention on the Status of Refugees – has been the lack of a well-defined system for responsibility sharing among states. Consequently, developing countries host the vast majority of the world's refugees, while developed countries' contributions to protection, assistance, and solutions fluctuate according to their political and economic priorities. In 2015, the United Nations High Commissioner's (UNHCR) Assistant High Commissioner for Protection described "the need for a global compact on predictable and equitable burden and responsibility-sharing" as "the most critical protection gap we are facing today."[12]

The Global Compact on Refugees, affirmed by the General Assembly in December 2018, goes some way towards addressing this gap. Though non-binding in a legal sense, it is an ambitious, forward-looking statement of political will. Significantly, it signals widespread recognition that the challenges facing the international refugee regime cannot be fully addressed without a more equitable distribution of responsibility among states (and other relevant actors) to support refugees and their host communities.[13]

The four stated objectives of the Global Compact on Refugees are to: ease the pressure on host countries, enhance refugee self-reliance, expand access to third-country solutions and support conditions in countries of origin for return in safety and dignity. It comprises of a Comprehensive Refugee Response Framework (CRRF), a Programme of Action and arrangements for follow-up and review. Given its non-binding nature, the Global Compact will be operationalised through voluntary contributions by states and other relevant stakeholders, taking capacity and national context into account.

The CRRF was agreed to by member states in Annex 1 of the New York Declaration.[14] It is designed to ensure (a) rapid and well-supported reception and admission measures; (b) support for immediate and ongoing needs (e.g. protection, health, and education); (c) assistance to national/local institutions and communities receiving refugees; and (d) expanded opportunities for durable solutions. The CRRF strives to benefit both refugees and host communities by involving a wide group of stakeholders, linking humanitarian and development efforts early on in a crisis, and expanding opportunities for durable solutions. UNHCR is already applying the CRRF in various national and regional refugee situations.[15]

The Programme of Action sets out concrete measures to help achieve the goals of the Global Compact. A Global Refugee Forum will be held every four years, at which all United Nations member states and relevant stakeholders will be invited to announce concrete pledges and contributions and explore how to enhance responsibility sharing. A Support Platform will also be established, to be activated for specific large-scale refugee situations in order to mobilise support, assistance, and action. The Programme of Action also describes the types of national and regional arrangements that could be adopted for specific situations and sets out tools that could be used to operationalise responsibility sharing.

The final element of the CRRF comprises arrangements for follow-up and review, namely the Global Refugee Forum, a high-level officials meeting held every two years between forums, and UNHCR's annual report to the General Assembly.

The development of the Global Compact on Refugees is a positive step forward in addressing the responsibility-sharing gap in the international protection regime, though it is too early for its full impact to be seen. Significantly, the Programme of Action is underpinned by age, gender, and diversity considerations, including promoting gender equality and empowering women and girls as well as ending all forms of sexual and gender-based violence, trafficking in persons, sexual exploitation and abuse and harmful practices.[16]

Where it counts: Implementation of the international protection regime

At the end of the day, whether binding or not, international instruments and tools are only as strong as their implementation. The decision whether to accede to, vote in support of, or otherwise indicate a willingness to commit to such instruments and tools – and, evidently, whether to implement them on the ground – rests with states. The real impact of the international refugee law framework, therefore, is always subject to political will.

Particularly in recent years, the world has watched as protectionist politics have overridden humanitarian imperatives time and time again. Anti-immigration sentiments, coupled with outright racism, are prevalent in many parts of the world (most notably the developed world). Asylum seekers and refugees are often associated more with economic and social disruption than humanitarian need. They are met with distrust and resentment rather than compassion and respect.

A widespread fear of "the other" is fuelled by biased, unrepresentative media coverage of migrants and refugees engaging in criminal behaviour, as well as the misleading comments of leading politicians. The general public is swayed to believe that refugees are somehow predisposed to violence and criminality.[17] This misinformation is further fuelled by assertions that asylum seekers enter (or seek to enter) developed countries illegally. It is not illegal to seek asylum under any circumstances.

White nationalism is on the rise, particularly owing to the links that are irresponsibly drawn – again by the media, right-wing politicians, and uninformed members of the public – between refugees and terrorism. Exclusionary attitudes and practices are particularly targeted at Muslim refugees.

So how does this exclusionary, anti-immigration discourse impact on the provision of protection to those in need?

The actions of developed states vary greatly and depend on national context. Some have tightened their migration policies and clamped down on the unregulated arrival of asylum seekers by imposing physical and/or administrative obstacles.[18] Several countries in Europe have reportedly deported asylum seekers.[19] Other states have reduced the number of refugees they accept through resettlement, or have limited their intake to certain religious or cultural groups.[20] Despite states' resettlement commitments in the 2016 New York Declaration, the UNHCR has reported that the growth in resettlement quotas over 2012–2016 saw "a steep reversal" in 2017, with only 75,200 refugees submitted for resettlement – less than half of the number submitted in the previous year.[21] With respect to responsibility sharing, Russia and the United States voted against the adoption of the Global Compact on Refugees in 2018, signaling an unwillingness to step up their efforts.[22] More drastically, some political leaders in Australia have even considered (or called for) withdrawal from the 1951 Convention.[23]

In light of the developed world's wavering commitment to providing protection and finding solutions, developing countries continue to host the majority of the world's refugees. Some do not have the resources, capacity and/or political will to implement their obligations in full. Specifically, with respect to women, this gives rise to the types of issues raised throughout this book such as insufficient protection against SGBV and limited access to education and employment. Of course, cultural barriers to women's rights also play a significant role in some countries, impacting on laws and policies (including refugee determination processes), as well as women's social, economic, and political participation.

Developments such as the Global Compact are important but must result in a more equitable distribution of refugees worldwide. Merely better resourcing the developing world to continue hosting the vast majority of the world's refugees is not a sign of true responsibility sharing, but rather indicates a desire for the developed world to keep the refugee "problem" out of sight.

Where to from here?

The picture is not all bleak. Footage from Germany in 2015 showed masses of Germans greeting trains brimming with refugees with signs and gifts of welcome. The 2014 "I'll ride with you" social media campaign, which started in Australia as a gesture of support for Muslims to combat racist backlash following a hostage crisis in Sydney, spread worldwide in a matter of days. Protests continue around the world in support of refugees and in objection to harsh policies that limit their prospects and protection, with individuals and communities demonstrating generosity and support through a range of innovative projects and initiatives.

Yet there is a long way to go before the positive efforts of a few translate into the lasting practice of many. Turning to the legal framework, the international community must continue to strive for universal accession to international refugee and human rights law instruments, as well as the removal of all reservations. Steps must continue to be taken to bolster the international regime with various soft law instruments as required. Significantly, the framework must be interpreted and implemented to the highest possible standard and in line with its objectives, in a sufficiently flexible way so as to adapt to the changing global context.

Improving standards of protection and access to durable solutions around the world inevitably depends on enhanced global responsibility sharing. The Global Compact on Refugees is a positive step in the right direction, not least as it makes some progress towards closing a critical gap in the international protection regime. Yet the willingness of states to accept a greater share of the global responsibility for refugee protection will depend on political will, which is largely driven by the demands of the general population.

In this light, efforts must be strengthened – particularly in developed countries – to increase the global population's awareness of the plight and rights of refugees, including the incontestable fact that it is not illegal to seek asylum. Refugees do not willfully leave their countries in search of a *better life*. They are forced to flee in search of *a life*. Crucially, refugees must be presented in a more positive light to the public eye, focusing on their skills and positive attributes, so that they are welcomed and embraced rather than excluded and vilified.

The key to social inclusion is enabling refugees to participate in the social and economic lives of their host countries as soon as possible after they arrive. Fear feeds on the unknown, and vicious stereotypes spread irrespective of their sources. Refugees must be empowered to receive an education, develop their skills, and give back to their communities through lawful employment. If refugees are seen, known, and valued as positive contributors, this will undoubtedly help to prevent or reduce tensions with their host communities. A shift away from policies that house refugees in camps – often a breeding ground for sexual and gender-based violence – can also give refugees more opportunities to contribute to their communities, both economically and socially.

More broadly, it must be recognised that while addressing the root causes of displacement is primarily the responsibility of the country(ies) involved, it is in the interest of the international community for cross-border displacement to not be triggered in the first place.[24] When large-scale displacement crises do occur, there is a need for more awareness about the social, economic, security, and political benefits of responding to the protection needs of refugees for individual countries, regions, and the world at large. When it comes to finding solutions to forced displacement, it must be recognised that this can help not only to resolve current situations but also to prevent future crises.[25]

As this book has shown, the lack of adequate refugee protection is a particular concern for women and girls. On International Women's Day 2019, the

UN Secretary General observed that there is a similar lack of political will with respect to the protection, promotion, and respect of women's rights, as discussed above in relation to the rights of refugees: "Everywhere around the world we see two parallel trends. While global movements and increased awareness are contributing to greater acknowledgement of the need for gender equality, this is happening simultaneously with a reinvigorated pushback on women's rights."[26]

Achieving gender equality and ensuring adequate protection for women and girl refugees is not just important at the level of individuals, families, and communities. For the world to make real progress towards the prevention and resolution of large-scale displacement crises, as well as the protection of displaced populations, gender equality must be at the forefront of all decisions and developments at national, regional, and international levels.

Notes

1 In 2017, there were 68.5 million forcibly displaced people worldwide, comprising 25.4 million refugees, 3.1 million asylum seekers and 40 million internally displaced people: UNHCR, "Global Trends: Forced Displacement in 2017," available at https://www.unhcr.org/globaltrends2017/ (last accessed February 9, 2020).
2 UNHCR notes that the gap between the needs of refugees and humanitarian funding has widened, and there is an urgent need for more equitable responsibility sharing: Report of the United Nations High Commissioner for Refugees, Part II Global compact on refugees, General Assembly A/73/12 (Part II) para 1.
3 Report of the United Nations High Commissioner for Refugees, Part II Global compact on refugees, General Assembly A/73/12 (Part II).
4 Universal Declaration of Human Rights 1948, article 14.
5 This is the principle of *non-refoulement*, which is at the core of international protection and is a norm of customary international law.
6 See UN General Assembly, *Convention Relating to the Status of Refugees*, July 28, 1951, United Nations, Treaty Series, vol. 189, p. 137, available at: https://www.refworld.org/docid/3be01b964.html (last accessed February 9, 2020).
7 See, for example, the Organisation of African Unity (now African Union) Convention governing the Specific Aspects of Refugee Problems in Africa 1969, adopted in Addis Adaba, September 10, 1969; the European Union Council Directive 2004/83/EC of April 29, 2004, on minimum standards for the qualification and status of third country nationals or stateless persons as refugees or as persons who otherwise need international protection and the content of the protection granted, Official Journal L 304, 30/09/2004 P. 0012 – 0023; and the non-binding Cartagena Declaration on Refugees, adopted at a colloquium held at Cartagena, Colombia, November 19–22, 1984.
8 Volker Türk and Rebecca Dowd, "Protection Gaps," The Oxford Handbook of Refugee and Forced Migration Studies, E. Fiddian-Qasmiyeh et al. (eds) (2014), p. 283.
9 For more details, see Volker Türk and Rebecca Dowd, "Protection Gaps," The Oxford Handbook of Refugee and Forced Migration Studies, E. Fiddian-Qasmiyeh et al. (eds) (2014), p. 283.
10 Report of the United Nations High Commissioner for Refugees, Part II Global compact on refugees, General Assembly A/73/12 (Part II) para 13.
11 For more details, see Volker Türk and Rebecca Dowd, "Protection Gaps," The Oxford Handbook of Refugee and Forced Migration Studies, E. Fiddian-Qasmiyeh et al. (eds) (2014), p. 283.

12 Statement by Volker Türk, Assistant High Commissioner for Protection' to the 66th Session of the Executive Committee of the High Commissioner's Programme, Agenda point 5(a) (October 8, 2015), available at: https://www.unhcr.org/admin/dipstatements/56150fb66/66th-sessionexecutive-committee-high-commissioners-programme-agenda-point.html (last accessed February 9, 2020).
13 The Global Compact on Refugees Guiding Principles states that it "represents the political will and ambition of the international community as a whole for strengthened cooperation and solidarity with refugees and affected host countries."
14 UN General Assembly, *New York Declaration for Refugees and Migrants: resolution / adopted by the General Assembly*, October 3, 2016, A/RES/71/1.
15 For more details, see UNHCR, "The New York Declaration for Refugees and Migrants: Responses to Frequently Asked Questions," p. 4, available at https://www.unhcr.org/584689257.pdf (last accessed February 9, 2020).
16 Report of the United Nations High Commissioner for Refugees, Part II Global compact on refugees, General Assembly A/73/12 (Part II) para 13.
17 For a discussion about fear-mongering towards Sudanese Australians, see Melanie Baak, "Sudanese heritage youth in Australia are frequently maligned by fear-mongering and racism," *The Conversation,* January 11, 2018, available at: https://theconversation.com/sudanese-heritage-youth-in-australia-are-frequently-maligned-by-fear-mongering-and-racism-89763 (last accessed February 9, 2020).
18 For example, in 2015, Hungary erected a tall fence between Hungary and Serbia that is topped with barbed wire and patrolled by police. It has been described as "one of the most fortified" borders in Europe: Shaun Walker, "No entry: Hungary's crackdown on helping refugees," *The Guardian Australia* online, June 4, 2018.
19 Judith Vonberg, "How some European countries are tightening their refugee policies," *CNN*, February 22, 2017.
20 For example, in 2015–2017, Australia's conservative coalition government preferred accepting Christian refugees from Syria and Iraq, despite this being a minority religion: A. Odysseus Patrick, "Australia's Immoral Preference for Christian Refugees," *The New York Times,* May 3, 2017.
21 UNHCR, "UNHCR projected global resettlement needs 2019," 24th Annual Tripartite Consultations on Resettlement, June 25–26, 2018.
22 Edith M. Lederer, "UN approves compact to support world's refugees; US objects," *AP News*, December 18, 2018, available at: https://www.apnews.com/4fd4c127e8da4801b6bb3f8d5f184404 (last accessed February 9, 2020).
23 The Australian Coalition Government considered withdrawal in 2013, and other conservative parties have called for withdrawal since: "Refugee Convention withdrawal 'an option'," *The Sydney Morning Herald online,* July 19, 2013, available at: https://www.smh.com.au/politics/federal/refugee-convention-withdrawal-an-option-20130719-2q7xs.html (last accessed February 9, 2020).
24 This is in line with the Global Compact on Refugees as well as the 2030 Agenda for Sustainable Development and the Sendai Framework for Disaster Risk Reduction 2015–2030.
25 Volker Türk, "66th Session of the Executive Committee of the High Commissioner's Programme Agenda point 5(a). Statement by Volker Türk, Assistant High Commissioner for Protection," October 8, 2015, available at https://www.unhcr.org/admin/dipstatements/56150fb66/66th-sessionexecutive-committee-high-commissioners-programme-agenda-point.html (last accessed February 9, 2020).
26 António Guterres, "Remarks on International Women's Day 2019, March 8, 2019," available at https://www.un.org/sg/en/content/sg/speeches/2019-03-08/womens-day-2019-remarks (last accessed February 9, 2020).

INDEX

Note: Page numbers followed by "n" denote endnotes.

adolescent girls, insecurities for 114
Afghanistan–Turkey–Greece, 2015 104–106
Afghan refugee 104–106
Age, Gender and Diversity Policy (2018) 16
Algeria: refugee camp in 25, 117, 156; West Saharan women in 56–61
Aliens and Nationality Law, Liberia 17
anti-immigration sentiments 172
Arendt, Hannah 10
asylum seekers 3, 9, 89, 129, 172; detention of 17; material deprivation of 3; protection of 171
AU Convention 138

Bangladesh, Rohingya women in 25–37
Beijing Platform for Action (1994) 20
Betts, Alexander 9

Cartagena Convention 138
Cartagena Declaration on Refugees (1984) 12
CEDAW *see* Convention on the Elimination of all forms of Discrimination Against Women (CEDAW)
Chowdhury, Shahanoor Akter 7
Cicero, Marcus Tillius 101
Citizenship Bill 17
civil society 10, 18, 144
Coddington, Kate 139

Code de la Nationalité, Togo 17
Common European Asylum System 12
Community Watch groups 125
complex cases 166–167
Comprehensive Refugee Response Framework (CRRF) 171
Conclusion on Refugee Women 5
conflict: role of 165–166; violent 127, 131, 134; *see also* violent conflict; women 119–120
conflict-induced displacements 119–120
Convention on the Elimination of all forms of Discrimination Against Women (CEDAW) 13, 20n5; adoption of 15–16
Cox's Bazar, Bangladesh: birth at 93; children learning 100; death at 98; refugee camps in 90–101, 120, 124; Rohingya refugee crisis in 123–124; Ukhiya refugee camp 152
Crabapple, Molly 7
crisis 3, 138; European refugee and migrant 14; of identity 7–8
CRRF *see* Comprehensive Refugee Response Framework (CRRF)

Dadaab Refugee Camp 128–129
decision-making processes 15, 25
de facto stateless persons 151
Democratic Republic of Congo (DRC) 111, 112; refugee women in 61–66
displaced and statelessness 152–154

178 Index

Doctors Without Borders/Médecins Sans Frontières (MSF) 72–73; birth in 84–87; cleaning woman at 88; health worker with expectant mother in 83
Dohuk Refugee Camp 74
domestic violence 14, 115, 120, 131; role of 165–166
Domiz camp, in Iraqi Kurdistan 72; refugee in 76
Dowd, Rebecca 8
Dryden-Peterson, Sarah 140

Eapen, Rebecca 4
education 140, 157, 169; role of 160–163
equality 15–16
Europe: refugees 14; Syrian family to leave for 75–76; Syrian refugees trip to 72–89
exile: family separation in 120–121; and opportunities 132–133
exploitation 137; in displacement 118; exposure to 154; stateless persons 153

family separation 82; in exile 120–121
feminists: Abeer 102–104; Biba 106–108; Shabana 104–106
forced displacement 112; levels of 19; of people in history 136; poverty and informality 137–140; protection challenges faced by women and girls in 14–16; statelessness 154
forced migrants 136, 143; opportunities for 137, 138; refugee camps 137
forced migration 112, 141–143; gender roles and relations 115
formal sector, economic opportunities in 130
Freedman, Jane 7

Gaddafi, Muammar 108
gang violence 14
gender-based violence (GBV) 5, 6, 14–16, 111; exposure to 154; strengthening strategies for change 16–17
gender discriminatory laws 150–151
gendered labour, within refugee 142
gendered nature of work 141–142
gender equality 18, 19, 125, 175
gender equality laws 17
gender inequality 14, 15, 111, 169–170
gender-integrated approach 125
Gerver, Mollie 8
Gleibet Lfoula camp 120–121
Global Action Network for the Forcibly Displaced 9
Global Action Plan to End Statelessness 17

global burden-sharing 144
Global Compact on Refugees (GCR) 5–6, 9, 18–19, 169, 170, 174; adoption of 172; development of 172; objectives of 171
Global North 144
Global Refugee Forum (GRF) 19, 171–172
global refugee system 3
Global South 128, 130, 132, 137
GRF *see* Global Refugee Forum (GRF)

Harakah al-Yaqin 26
harassment: sexual 121, 124, 132; stateless persons 153
healthcare, role of 164–165
host country fatigue 128–130

#IBelong Campaign to End Statelessness 17
identity crisis 7–8
"included exclusion" 129
India: Pakistani displaced minorities in 48–56; Sri Lankan Tamil women in 37–48
Indra, Doreen 141
informality 140; forced displacement 137–140
informal sector, economic opportunities in 130
insecurity 131–132; for adolescent girls 114
inter-agency assessment report 14
Intergovernmental Panel on Refugees and Displaced Persons 9–10
internally displaced persons (IDPs) 3, 15
internally displaced women, in Syria: Ghadeer Haytham Al-Sett 69; Mirvat Saleem Naqqar 66–69; Samira Mahmoud Arnaout 69–71
international human rights framework 156
international protection regime 169; implementation of 172–173
international refugee law 13–14; framework 170–172
intimate partner violence 6, 15

Jaji, Rose 7

Kakuma refugee camp, in Kenya 162–163
Kannan, Sweta Madhuri 4
Kenya 128–129; Kakuma refugee camp in 162–163
Kurdish Syrian refugees 72

livelihoods: destruction of 128; role of 163–164; South Sudanese women 163–164

Macedonia, refugee camp in 104

National Commission for Refugees (CNR) 64, 65
nationality 149, 154–155; acquisition of 151
nationality laws 150
national legislation 169–170
New York Declaration 171, 173
New York Declaration for Refugees and Migrants 9, 13
Niger–Libya, 2010 106–108
non-governmental organisations (NGOs) 19, 31–32, 111, 113, 133

opportunities: employment 169; exile and 132–133; for forced migrants 137, 138; for Syrian refugees 139
Organization of African Unity (OAU) Convention governing Specific Aspects of Refugee Problems in Africa (1969) 12

Pakistani displaced minorities, in India: Balwanti 55–56; Jamuna 52–53; Khushboo 53–54, 114, 139; Mala 50–51; Ragini 54–55; Suman Devi 48–49, 139, 140
physical violence 132
polygamy 124
poverty 130, 134, 136, 137; forced displacement 137–140
Programme of Action 170–172
protection: lack of 111; and prevention strategies 124; within refugee camps 113; standards of 174; for women girl refugees 175
protection gaps, for women and girls 111–117
protracted displacement 136

rape 111, 119, 155
refugee camps: across Asia and Africa 4; in Cox's Bazar, Bangladesh 90–101; forced migrants 137; in Macedonia 104; protection within 113; Rohingya women in 120; violence and insecurities of life in 113
Refugee Convention (1951) 9, 12, 13, 138, 157, 171
Refugee Convention (1967) 138

refugee policies 10
refugee protection 174–175
refugees: defined as 12; international protection framework for 13; international protection of 12; interpretation of 170; material deprivation of 3; object of discourse 8–11; perception of 134; representation in media 5; strengthening strategies for change 16–17; see also women
refugee system 10
refugee women 25; and difficulties 130–132; special vulnerability of 5–6; stereotypical depiction of 133
refugee women, in DRC: Amina Tabeya 63–64, 121; Jacqueline Habonimana 64–65; Malaika 61–62, 113–116, 139; Ruth 62–63, 112, 115–117; Safi Misago 65–66, 122, 123
returnees 15–16
Rohingya exodus (2017) 90–101
Rohingya people 152, 159n25
Rohingya refugees, displaced families in refugee camps 113
Rohingya women, in Bangladesh 25, 125; Anowara 29–30; Ayesha 36–37; Ayesha Begum 28, 115; Firoza Khatun 28–29; Khurshida 36–37; Laila Begum 36–37; Majeda 30–31; Murshida 31–32; Noor Bibi 26–28; Nurunnahar 32–33; Rahima 33–34, 138–139; Roshida Begum 35–36, 111–112, 114, 116

safe spaces 124–125
Sahrawi Arab Democratic Republic 151
Sahrawi/Western Saharan people 151, 156
Sanyal, Romola 8
self-reliance, quest for 133–134
self-sufficiency 128, 135
sexual abuse 131
sexual and gender-based violence (SGBV) 111–113, 122, 127, 131, 132, 174; protection against 173
sexual and reproductive health and rights (SRHR) violations 15
sexual harassment 121, 124, 132
sexual violence 6, 7, 111–112, 114–115, 124
Shandilya, Divita 8
Shilpi, Sharmin Akther 7
single women 120–121, 124
social inclusion 174
Somalia, Citizenship Bill 17
South Sudanese women 160–162; conflict 165–166; domestic violence 165–166;

180 Index

education 160–163; healthcare 164–165; livelihoods 163–164
Sri Lankan Tamil women, in India: Jayapriya 40–41, 123; Jensy Niraja 43–45, 139, 141, 142; Padma Jothi 37–40, 139, 142; Ramana Devi 41–43; Rohini 45–46, 112; Tharani 46–48
statelessness 158; in abeyance 154–156; and displaced 153–154, 157; making of 150–153
stateless person 149–155, 157, 158
structural violence 143
Support Platform 172
Sur, Priyali 7
Sustainable Development Goals 19
Syrian refugees: crisis 72; displaced families in refugee camps 113; internally displaced women in 66–71; opportunities for 139; statelessness 155; trip to Europe 72–89
Syria–Turkey–Greece–North Macedonia–Serbia–the Hungarian border, 2015 102–104

Tanzania 128
trafficking 118, 121
transience fallacy 128–130
trauma 119–120, 131; healing from 134
Türk, Volker 176n12

United Nations High Commissioner for Refugees (UNHCR) 5, 12–16, 19, 20n1, 111–113, 155, 157, 170; stateless persons estimation 150
United Nations Relief and Works Agency for Palestine Refugees (UNWRA) 155
UN Security Council 111

violence 108, 119–120; and insecurity 131; by non-state actors against women 14; outbreak of 152
violent conflict 127, 131, 134; destruction of livelihoods 128
vulnerability: affect forced migrants 137; of refugee women 5–6

Water, Sanitation and Hygiene (WASH) groups 125
West Saharan women, in Algeria: Bintou 56–57, 141; Lalla 57–58; Maoualmin 58–59, 119, 120; Maymouna 59–61, 120–123
women: conflict, violence, and trauma 119–120; family separation in exile 120–121; invisibility in host country 121–123; multi-faceted social and cultural isolation of 118–126; *see also* refugees
women asylum seekers, detention of 17
women with disabilities 125
Women's Refugee Commission 114
World Health Organisation (WHO) 119
World Refugee Council 3, 9

Printed in the USA
CPSIA information can be obtained
at www.ICGtesting.com
LVHW010225110224
771451LV00003B/299